Welcome
to the
Church
of the
Nazarene

WELCOME

to the

CHURCH

of the

NAZARENE

An Introduction to Membership

Nazarene Publishing House
Kansas City, Missouri

Contents

"The Church of the Nazarene
has set its face toward the
northern star of
perfect love
and will not swerve
to the right
or to the left."
—Dr. Phineas F. Bresee

Foreword

I am happy to commend to you this handbook to prepare persons for meaningful membership in the Church of the Nazarene. It is not only biblically and theologically correct; it is also eminently understandable and practical. Although designed primarily for those without previous acquaintance with our church, those who are already members will profit by the reading of these pages.

The historical section traces the origin of the Church of the Nazarene in the great revival that spread throughout the United States following the Civil War. At the heart of this revival was the truth of scriptural holiness, which John Wesley recovered for the Church: the message that sinners can be saved from the guilt and power of sin through faith in Jesus Christ, and that Christian believers can be cleansed by faith from the corruption of remaining sin in their hearts and filled with God's perfect love. It was out of this revival that the Church of the Nazarene came into existence under the ministry of Dr. Phineas F. Bresee in 1895 in Los Angeles.

"Getting the glory down" was a phrase coined by Dr. Bresee. The early Nazarenes were characterized by this "glory," the manifestation of the Holy Spirit in their midst. Essential to maintaining this "glory" is commonality of faith, spirit, and lifestyle. The goal of Christian experience, as these pages make clear, is perfect love (John Wesley's favorite term for the experience of heart holiness). But perfect love can be maintained only in "the unity of the Spirit" (Eph. 4:3). This unity of the Spirit presupposes both agreement on the essentials in doctrine and commitment to a lifestyle that witnesses to and sustains total commitment to the Lordship of Christ.

There is in the Church of Jesus Christ "such . . . fellowship as cannot otherwise be known." To enjoy this fellowship—the word is *koinōnia* in the New Testament—we must be of one mind and heart. It is my hope and prayer that as you read these pages and attend the class in church membership, you will decide that the Church of the Nazarene is that part of Christ's Body you wish to join and support.

—WILLIAM M. GREATHOUSE
General Superintendent Emeritus

1

Introducing the Church of the Nazarene

Welcome to the Church of the Nazarene. You may be taking a class because you are planning to join the church. Perhaps you are reading this booklet because you would like to learn more about the church before you make a decision concerning membership. Or you may simply be interested in learning about the church that you attend. It is our hope that God will meet your needs in these lessons.

The Outline of Our Study

There are five areas of study that we will look at together. The subjects are:

1. *Where We Come From.* A brief survey of the early history and the beginning of the Church of the Nazarene.

- The Church of the Nazarene was born in the spirit of revival.
- The Church of the Nazarene was born in the spirit of unity.
- The Church of the Nazarene was born in the spirit of great people.
- The Church of the Nazarene was born in the Spirit of God.

2. *What We Believe.* A look at the beliefs, doctrines, and central teachings of our church.

- A statement of belief
- Living out our beliefs
- The place of doctrine

3. *How We Are Organized.* An overview of the leaders, finances, and ministries of the church.

- How we are organized through leadership
- How we are organized financially
- How we are organized for ministry

4. *How We Live as Christians.* An understanding of our positive approach to Christian discipline and living in the love of God.

- Building on the right foundation
- A positive attitude toward discipline
- A social stand through discipline
- The Christ-filled goal of discipline

5. *What It Means to Be a Church Member.* A practical guide for becoming a member of the church.

- A church of opportunity
- A church of responsibility
- Joining the Church of the Nazarene

At the end of these studies, you will be given an opportunity to express your desire to join the church. However, you are already welcome as part of our fellowship.

By Way of Introduction

The church is not composed simply of statements of doctrine, ethical stands, organization, or buildings and institutions. The church is people.

Nazarenes are people with a common desire to be all God wants them to be. You will find Nazarenes around the world.

[The Church of the Nazarene] is not a mission, but a church with a mission. It is a banding together of hearts that have found the peace of God, and which now in their gladness, go out to carry the message of the unsearchable riches of the Gospel of Christ to other suffering, discouraged, sin-sick souls.

—Flyer, Church of the Nazarene, 1895

If you want to know about the Church of the Nazarene, it is essential that you get close to the people who call themselves Nazarenes. We are ordinary people from all walks of life who serve an extraordinary God who is teaching us to walk in the Spirit.

If you are reading this booklet as part of a membership class, take a few moments and begin to get acquainted with the others in your class. If you are reading this booklet individually, remember that while the church can be explained in a written form, it can only be experienced in the people with whom you work and serve.

The church is a family. It is a way of thinking. It is a way of responding to the joys and hurts that we share together. There is an old hymn that describes the church as a family. We have "kindred minds."

Blest be the tie that binds
Our hearts in Christian love;
The fellowship of kindred minds
Is like to that above.

Before our Father's throne
We pour our ardent prayers;
Our fears, our hopes, our aims are one,
Our comforts and our cares.

We share our mutual woes,
Our mutual burdens bear;
And often for each other flows
The sympathizing tear.

—JOHN FAWCETT

Describing the Church of the Nazarene

Let us share with you six statements that characterize our church. These statements tell you who we are and what we are striving for.

1. *The Church of the Nazarene is characterized by a great spirit of positive enthusiasm and anticipation concerning its pastor, its members, its programs, and its ministry.*

We are a people who anticipate every Sunday with delight rather than drudgery. It is not simply obligation but excitement and joy that bring us together. We desire to maintain a positive feeling of faith concerning the programs and ministries that are designed to meet the needs of the people, in the home and in the church.

2. *The Church of the Nazarene uses every imaginative method possible to meet the needs of people and bring them into a personal relationship with Jesus Christ as Lord and Master of their lives.*

Our methods are flexible, but our message is stable: "Jesus is Lord." We want to use our God-given imagination and complete trust in Him to meet the needs of people with the love of Christ. We are always asking the question, "What do we need to be doing?"

3. *The Church of the Nazarene is comfortable with its framework of belief and organization.*

Doctrine, at its best, is our explanation of God's love. It is never exhaustive, but expressive of what we have experienced. The test of doctrine is faithfulness to the Bible and fruitfulness in meeting the needs of people. We believe that life can be meaningful and fulfilling through a personal relationship with Jesus Christ.

Concerning organization, there are no perfect systems. However, this does not release us from the need for organization and structure. Our system puts faith in the laity and the clergy, faith that is built on the attitude of unity and love.

4. *The Church of the Nazarene views money as a means to an end, not an end in itself.*

In our church the bottom line is not money, but ministry. We refuse to be bound by the pressure of allowing finances to become more important than they really are. We believe that good communication, genuine integrity, and a need-centered program will inspire people who are sensitive to the leading of God as they give cheerfully and enthusiastically.

5. *The Church of the Nazarene has a deep commitment to meeting the needs of people, which results naturally in a growing church.*

The only reason we count *people* is because people *count*. A congregation that believes in the faith, hope, and love of the Bible will strive to meet people where they are with what they need. We believe that if needs are being met, the church will grow.

6. *The Church of the Nazarene is committed to providing adequate physical facilities to care for an expanding pattern of growth, and to involving increasing numbers of laypeople in the church's work.*

We believe that an adequate building is necessary for a great work. However, it is far more important to have people who are willing to work. We believe in providing opportunities of service and a ministry for every person who desires to participate in God's kingdom. The pastor's job is "to prepare God's people for works of service" (Eph. 4:12). Whatever your talents, whatever your dreams, whatever your abilities, whatever your interests, there is a place for you in the advancement of the work of the Lord.

2

Where We Come From

During a General Assembly (the meeting every four years of representatives and interested members from Nazarene churches around the world), the streets of Kansas City were overrun with thousands of Nazarenes. They filled the hotels and restaurants and city sidewalks. Their enthusiasm, excitement, and close-knit family feeling identified them.

In the midst of this enormous gathering, a man who had no connection with any church sat in a shoeshine parlor looking in disbelief at this great group of people and said, "Who are these Nazarenes?"

The man shining his shoes answered directly, and without hesitation, "Well, they're sort of souped-up Methodists."

1. It is true that the Church of the Nazarene is rooted in the teaching of John Wesley, the founder of Methodism.

2. Most of the founders came from Methodist backgrounds, but some came from other denominations.

The Church of the Nazarene Was Born in the Spirit of Revival

In the aftermath of the Civil War, a spiritual awakening infiltrated the sod houses of the prairie, the fine brick homes of New England, the plantations and shantytowns of the Deep South, and the religious heart of the nation.

The Crisis Experience of the Revival

The central thrust of this great revival was the fullness of God's powerful love. Dwight L. Moody heard a young man preach for six nights in a row on John 3:16. Moody's reaction was, "I never knew up to that time that God loved us so much. This heart of mine began to thaw out. I knew I could not keep back the tears. It was like news from a far country; I just drank it in." The nation was drinking in the perfect love of God.

Evangelist Moody, while holding a meeting in Chicago in 1871, was approached by two godly women who announced that they were praying for him. Moody exclaimed, "Why don't you pray for the people? I am all right."

To this they answered, "You are not all right. You do not have power."

Moody was upset by this at first, but in time he began to desire the powerful love these women were praying for. Later he gave this testimony: "They continued to pray for me; the result was that at the end of three months, God sent this blessing upon me, and I could not for the world go back to where I was before 1871."

John S. Inskip, a great preacher and evangelist, refers to the turning point in his life. "I was preaching on 'Let us lay aside every weight' [Heb. 12:1, KJV], and I heard a voice within say, 'Do it yourself and do it now.' I then stated to my congregation, 'Come, brethren, follow your pastor. I call heaven and earth to witness that I now declare I will henceforth wholly and forever be the Lord's!'" Powerful, pure love changed his ministry.

Charles G. Finney, whose meetings and messages were known across the United States, tells us of his crisis experience. "No words can express the wonderful love that was shed abroad in my heart. I wept aloud with joy."

The ancient truth of the Bible was coming to light in our own country: Christians can truly be holy, happy, victorious, love-filled children of God.

The Consequences of the Revival

By the turn of the century, tens of thousands of people had found this gift of heart purity and perfect love.

1. Several denominations had grown and expanded under the influence of the revival.

2. The revival gave rise to new colleges, Bible schools, and other training centers.
3. The revival also gave birth to several denominations. The largest of the classically Wesleyan-Holiness denominations is the Church of the Nazarene.

The Church of the Nazarene Was Born in the Spirit of Unity

During this same period of time, significant groups throughout the United States were discovering the biblical truth that a Christian can be cleansed and filled by God. They were learning that God's Holy Spirit can bring perfect love. These groups found a spirit of unity among themselves, joined together, and formed the Church of the Nazarene.

The Spirit Was Moving

During the years surrounding the turn of the century, people in many parts of the nation formed churches that were called to share the good news of heart cleansing and a life of holiness.

In New England. On May 12, 1886, a number of Christians in Providence, R.I., organized weekly services. They had discovered that they had a common experience of entire sanctification and wanted to promote this biblical teaching. After meeting in a private home for a few months, they rented a store. They organized a Sunday School and in July of 1887 became a church with 51 members. Rev. F. A. Hillery was their pastor.

A few months later, outside of Boston in Lynn, Mass., another church with a similar experience and interest was founded. Rev. C. Howard Davis was the pastor. Soon it was discovered that several churches of like interest and teaching had been started in southern New England.

Communications between these churches resulted in a union involving 10 congregations that took place on March 13-14, 1890. There in Rock, Mass., Rev. W. C. Ryder, a pastor, was elected as president. More churches were organized. It was a growing movement.

In New York City. In January of 1894, William Howard Hoople, a businessman in New York City, founded a mission in Brooklyn. He also wished to promote the teaching and experience of perfect love. In just five months an independent church was organized with 32 members. Mr. Hoople was called as its pastor.

Within the year, Hoople organized two other congregations in Brooklyn, and these three churches united in late 1895, forming a constitution and a summary of their teaching. Working with Rev. Hoople were Revs. H. B. Hosley, John Norberry, Charles H. BeVier, and H. F. Reynolds.

The group from the Boston area and the group from Brooklyn formed a joint committee. On November 12, 1896, the group agreed to join forces and resources in spreading the scriptural truth of holiness.

In Los Angeles. In October of 1895, a number of persons, under the leadership of Rev. Phineas F. Bresee, D.D., and J. P. Widney, M.D., formed the First Church of the Nazarene in Los Angeles.

Within 10 years, there were 26 organized congregations. And these were in great cities: Los Angeles; Oakland; Berkeley, Calif.; Seattle; Spokane, Wash.; Boise, Idaho; Salt Lake City; Omaha; and Chicago. At the October 1905 assembly, it was reported that there were 3,195 members.

In addition to churches and numbers, Dr. Bresee was collecting an impressive group of leaders: L. B. Kent and Isaiah Reid, veterans of the holiness movement in Illinois and Iowa; C. W. Ruth, evangelist from the Holiness Christian Church; C. E. Cornell, Friends lay evangelist from Cleveland; W. C. Wilson, formerly a Methodist evangelist in Kentucky; and John W. Goodwin, from New England.

In Tennessee and Texas. In 1894 at Milan, Tenn., the New Testament Church of Christ was organized by Rev. R. L. Harris with 14 members. Again, this was a group who found a common experience in the heart-cleansing power of God's love. The influence of this church spread throughout western Texas and Arkansas.

Another denomination, the Independent Holiness Church, was started in 1901 at Van Alstyne, Tex., by Rev. C. B. Jernigan. Within two years, this fast-growing organization had organized 20 churches. These two groups met in November 1904 and framed a *Manual* and a statement of their beliefs. A year later, they joined to become one group, the Holiness

Church of Christ. By 1908 it had nearly 75 churches throughout the South.

Unity Through God's Spirit

From these groups in diverse parts of the nation came the Church of the Nazarene. It was a joining of east and west, north and south.

As the group from the East and the group from the West came to know each other better, the feeling grew that they should unite. From their conference a statement was developed and unanimously adopted that expressed the real purpose of the church:

It is agreed that the two churches are one in the doctrines considered essential to salvation, especially the doctrines of justification by faith and entire sanctification subsequent to justification, also by faith, and as a result, the precious experience of entire sanctification as a normal condition of the churches. Both churches recognize that the right of church membership rests upon experience and that persons who have been born of the Spirit are entitled to its privileges.

The first assembly of the two churches was held in Chicago in October 1907. At that assembly, several representatives from the group in Tennessee and Texas accepted an invitation to attend. Talks concerning the union with the group began. A year later the assembly was held in Pilot Point, Tex., at the invitation of the Southern group. It was an amazing turn of events and an even more amazing turn of hearts that caused people from east and west, north and south to lay aside their differences so that God's kingdom might advance.

R. B. Mitchum moved: "That the union of the two churches be now consummated." On Tuesday, October 13, 1908, at 10:40 A.M., amid great shouts of joy and anticipation, the motion to unite was unanimously adopted. This date marks the beginning of the denomination of the Church of the Nazarene.

Other groups came to join the young denomination. Rev. J. O. McClurkan headed a group of very missionary minded people who also shared the same beliefs as the Nazarenes. In 1915 this group and their mission work joined the church. At the same time, a group of churches in the British Isles under the leadership of Rev. George Sharpe also became part of the Church of the Nazarene. Seven years later, the Laymen's Holiness Association of more than 1,000 members under the leadership of their president, Rev. J. G. Morrison, united with the Church of the Nazarene, bringing their extensive program of evangelism and camp meetings.

It is this same spirit of unity that still welcomes people from all over the world into the family of the Church of the Nazarene.

The Church of the Nazarene Was Born in the Spirit of Great People

God moves through the sweeping work of His Spirit in national revival and awakening. God moves through the unity of His people who set aside prejudices to be joined to His purpose. God also moves through individuals who are wholly committed to Him in all things.

The story of the Church of the Nazarene contains the stories of many, many great men and women of God: F. A. Hillery, W. C. Ryder, William Howard Hoople, H. F. Reynolds, Bud Robinson, C. W. Ruth, Rev. Mary Lee Cagle, C. B. Jernigan, J. G. Morrison, H. Orton Wiley, J. B. Chapman, R. T. Williams, Fairy Chism, E. P. Ellyson, and others.

The following is one story of many. It is the story of Dr. Phineas F. Bresee, the first person selected by the Church of the Nazarene to be one of its general superintendents. It is one story that demonstrates what God was doing across the nation at the time the Church of the Nazarene was born.

The Beginning. Phineas F. Bresee was born in a log cabin in Franklin, N.Y., on New Year's Eve in 1838. He was converted in February 1856. When the family moved to Iowa, this young man of 19 received a preacher's license. In 1861 he was ordained an elder in the Methodist church.

Early Pastorates. As a circuit rider, the young preacher was at first embittered and then challenged by his assignment. He said, "It should go; live or die, it should go." At the end of the first year, he had received 140 people into membership and purchased a comfortable parsonage as well as a fine buggy with a team of horses to take him to the conference.

As was the custom of the day, he moved to several churches, some for more than one term.

In these early years he developed two ideas that stayed with him all his life: (1) he used the custom of singing popular choruses in the song services; and (2) he reached the conviction that a large and beautiful building was unnecessary to any successful gospel work.

A Spiritual Search. The winter of 1866-67 was the beginning of a long search by Phineas Bresee. He writes, "It seemed as though I doubted everything." At a prayer meeting on a snowy night, from the altar of his own church, he prayed that the Lord would give him what he needed: He experienced the infilling presence of God's perfect love.

Yet his deeper relationship with God was to leave him for a time. His complete commitment to Christ was being challenged. Other things grew out of proper proportion.

Losing Sight of the Goal. Perhaps the major reason the experience of perfect love was lost was because of Bresee's involvement in an ill-fated gold mining venture in New Mexico. He became involved with a Rev. Joseph Knotts, a former pastor turned speculator in the gold mining business.

In 1879 Bresee took a rather insignificant church so that he might have more time to work on these enterprises. He even sold shares in the mine to his church members. Soon after this, there was a blast set off in the mine, and all the tools and machinery were destroyed. Bresee was in financial ruin and disgrace.

He learned his lesson. He determined that he would give the remainder of his life to the direct preaching of the Word of God. His friend Knotts gave him $1,000, and in 1883, at the age of 44, Bresee and his family of seven children and two grandparents boarded an "immigrant railway car" for California.

The New Beginning. The family arrived in Los Angeles, and the following Sunday Bresee was invited to preach at the First Methodist Church. He was installed as pastor within two weeks. There he encountered people in his fine church who understood the concept of allowing God to fill a Christian with His Holy Spirit and perfect love. He writes, "I instinctively, in spirit, allied myself with them."

Two men, McDonald and Watson, leading evangelists in

the National Holiness Association, conducted special services at the church for three weeks in 1884. It was in these services that Bresee settled once and for all the question of his complete commitment to the cleansing love of Jesus Christ. It was purity and power combined. Rarely does he tell about the experience, but on one occasion he put down in words: "There came into my heart and being a transformed condition of life and blessing and unction and glory, which I have never known before. I felt that my need was supplied."

From that point on, his ministry expanded greatly. Two years later, when he left the church at Los Angeles, the congregation had 650 members, four times that of any other in southern California, and they had well over 1,000 for every Sunday morning worship service.

The Age of Church Growth. In August 1886, Bresee was appointed to Pasadena, a little town in the foothills of the San Gabriel Mountains. The church had only 130 members. Bresee said, "By the grace of God, I am going to make a fire that will reach heaven."

By the end of the first year, the membership more than doubled. During the next six months, 250 members joined the church. They now had to build a tabernacle that would seat 2,000 people. The number of members stood at 700 by the end of the second year.

In 1891 Bresee was appointed presiding elder of the Los Angeles District. He stepped out to conduct a two-year campaign with meetings in every church in the area. These meetings across the city and throughout southern California produced great growth, excitement, and enthusiasm in all the churches.

A Test of Faith. Upon returning to southern California, John H. Vincent was presiding as bishop. He was an opponent of the holiness movement that Dr. Bresee was promoting. He removed Dr. Bresee from his office and appointed him as pastor of the Simpson Tabernacle in Los Angeles.

The church had a seating capacity of 2,500 people and finer acoustical arrangements than any theater or opera house in the state. However, the congregation was small and unable to pay off its debts. Within a year, they had to sell the building and close the church.

Not to be defeated, Dr. Bresee spent much of his time holding camp meeting services on other districts. Also, he became involved in supporting the recently founded University of Southern California in cooperation with J. P. Widney, M.D., a great friend.

Increasingly Bresee turned to an old dream for an inner-city mission to poor people. However, he could not get an appointment to this position through the Methodist church.

Dr. Bresee joined the Peniel Mission in 1894. This was a nondenominational mission, where he worked without an appointment. He would hold Tuesday prayer meetings, the Sunday morning service, and Friday night young people's meetings. Eventually he came to differ with the mission's founders over strategy. Bresee came to believe that the poor needed a full-fledged church of their own, but Peniel Mission's founders wanted to keep the focus of ministry on mission work. In 1895, when he made a journey to the Midwest to hold meetings and study the various missions of Chicago, the founders of the Peniel Mission dismissed him. At the age of 56, he was without a church, pulpit, or place to minister.

A New Church. Dr. Widney and Dr. Bresee began a new church on Sunday, October 6, 1895. Dr. Bresee's morning text was, "Thus saith the LORD, Stand ye in the ways, and see, and ask for the old paths, where is the good way, and walk therein, and ye shall find rest for your souls" (Jer. 6:16, KJV).

Two weeks later, 82 persons united as charter members of the Church of the Nazarene. Within a short time, that number had grown to 135. Most of these were new converts.

It was Dr. Widney who explained the name of the church. He said, "The word 'Nazarene' depicts the toiling, lowly mission of Christ. It was this name that was used in derision of Him by His enemies. It is this name that links Him with the struggling, sorrowing heart of the world. It is Jesus, Jesus of Nazareth, to whom the world in its misery and despair turns, that it may have hope."

The first piece of literature produced by the church reads: "Its mission is to everyone upon whom the battle of life has been sore and to every heart that hungers for cleansing from sin."

By the end of the first year, there were 350 members in

the church. Within eight years, there were 1,500 members in churches that stretched as far east as Illinois.

Four years later, the union that took place at Pilot Point, Tex., set a course for the Church of the Nazarene to become a worldwide denomination.

The Church of the Nazarene Was Born in the Spirit of God

It is interesting to note that the early characteristics of this church are the ideals that we set for our church today. The church's early history is recorded by Dr. Timothy L. Smith. He outlines the following:

The government of the church was to be thoroughly democratic. It is fully believed that God can work out His will through people who are committed to Him in love.

The chief aim of the church was to preach this message of holiness. Our holy God has come to make His people holy by cleansing from sin and filling with perfect love. Sharing this message was, and still is, the major mission of our church.

The discipline in the early church was dependent primarily upon the work of the Holy Spirit. Dr. Bresee always believed that if men and women were filled with God's love, the Holy Spirit could guide them in choosing a life that pleased God.

The church's statement of belief was central and made the concept of God's holy love most important. The church was to have no new doctrine, just old, old truth. It was not and is not a sect, splinter group, or anything other than a vehicle to preach and teach the biblical truth of holy love.

The church was characterized by a spirit that was joyously free. Whether they were worshiping on Sunday, calling through the week, meeting together for prayer meeting, or just going about their daily routine, there was a spirit of joyous freedom that was a part of these people and that is still with us today.

For many Nazarenes, Dr. Bresee characterizes the Church of the Nazarene. His pulpit delivery was conversational, speaking to each one as if he or she were the only one present. Regardless of the time of day, he always greeted people with "Good morning." It was a positive message. He even refused to park his buggy where he would have to back up. He wanted always to be moving ahead.

On Friday, October 8, 1915, Dr. Bresee attended his last General Assembly. He was again elected general superintendent. They presented him with 77 roses, one for each of the years of his life and one additional white rose for the year ahead. The rose was prophetic. Twenty-nine days after the assembly his lifework was finished.

His final formal message, written to his church, was Matt. 5:44-45: "Love your enemies and pray for those who persecute you, that you may be sons of your Father in heaven."

3

What We Believe

The Christian faith is more than an emotional experience; it also involves certain beliefs about God, ourselves, and our relationship to Him. It is part of the responsibility of the church to pass these beliefs on to its members in order to preserve the "faith that was once for all entrusted to the saints" (Jude 3). Paul was concerned that this be done (see 1 Cor. 15:1-4; 1 Tim. 3:9; 2 Tim. 2:2). The earliest Christian creed was both a statement of doctrine and an acknowledgment that brought salvation; it was "Jesus is Lord" (Rom. 10:9).

This shows that Christian beliefs are not merely intellectual in nature but point to truths that make possible our right relation to God. This is the point of the *Manual*'s statement concerning the central beliefs of the church that are "essential to Christian experience."

In the process of time it becomes important for a church to declare its beliefs on many matters. This is what the Church of the Nazarene has done. However, the church has taken great care to express beliefs that are clearly taught in Scripture. In this chapter, we will examine the church's beliefs and show how these beliefs relate to our Christian experience and daily living.

A Statement of Belief

The Church of the Nazarene has 16 Articles of Faith. These statements are printed at the end of this chapter.

A statement of doctrine is typically presented in the precise and technical language of theology. Here is a summary of these 16 statements:

1. We believe in one God, the Creator of all things, who reveals himself as Father, Son, and Spirit.
2. We believe in Jesus Christ, who is fully God and fully

man at the same time, who became like us to bring about our salvation.

3. We believe in the Holy Spirit, who is active in the world, bringing us to salvation.

4. We believe that the Bible is the Word of God, giving us all we need to know about how to be saved.

5. We believe that we are all sinners by both nature and act and need God's forgiveness and cleansing.

6. We believe that Jesus Christ died on the Cross and that, by trusting in His death, we can be restored to a right relation to God.

7. We believe that God has enabled us to turn to Him from sin but that He has not forced us to do so.

8. We believe that each person must repent, turn away from sin, and trust Christ to accept him or her.

9. We believe that when we turn from sin and trust in Christ, the old record of sin is wiped clean, and we are born anew, thus becoming part of the family of God.

10. We believe that after being born anew, we need the fullness of God's Spirit in our hearts. When we make a complete commitment to Him, He cleanses our spirit, fills us with His perfect love, and gives us the power to live victoriously.

11. We believe that the Church is the Body of Christ, carrying on His mission through the power of the Holy Spirit.

12. We believe in baptism and urge people to be baptized as Christians.

13. We believe in the Lord's Supper.

14. We believe that God can heal. We pray for healing. We also believe that He can work through medical science.

15. We believe that Jesus Christ is coming again.

16. We believe that everyone will face the judgment of God with its rewards and punishments.

A statement of belief has little value without the action of believing. To believe is to trust God, to trust Him with complete obedience.

God created a perfect world. That world included human

beings, Adam and Eve. This lovely world was maintained by God's simple plan, "You must not eat from the tree of the knowledge of good and evil, for when you eat of it you will surely die" (Gen. 2:17). God reserved the right to be God.

However, sin slipped in like a snake in the grass. The temptation was plain: "You will not surely die," the serpent said (Gen. 3:4). The temptation was: You cannot trust God; you must choose for yourself what is good and what is evil; "You will be like God" (v. 5).

We swallowed the line and have been choking on it ever since. The choice is very simple: If you cannot trust God to be your God, then you have your own god. And human beings were simply not designed for this. This is sin in our nature that is expressed in many sins of attitude and action.

God has not turned His back on us. He comes to bring us back to himself. Christ "came to seek and save what was lost" (Luke 19:10). He said, "I stand at the door and knock" (Rev. 3:20). God wants to truly be God, to decide what is good and what is bad for you.

We cannot turn over our lives to Him unless we trust Him in His love for us. God is seeking to win your trust. As amazing as it sounds, the God who created all things, this wonderful God, as Father, Son, and Spirit, is seeking to win your love, your confidence, and your obedience.

The Father seeks your love through the sending of His Son. In Jesus, God has put on our skin, become like us, walked into our world as one who loves us. The birth of Jesus proves that God is a good Father who can be trusted. The death of Jesus demonstrates the full extent of God's suffering love for us. And the resurrection of Jesus declares that God has done and can do all He promises.

The greatest love is the love between the Father and the Son. This living love is personified in the Holy Spirit. God sends the Spirit into our world today. He circles your life, moving, coaxing, wooing you. The moment you open your life in trust, the Spirit slips through the entrance, and you have entered into the love of God. In that moment, all sins are forgiven, the record of sins is erased, and you are adopted into the love of God.

The Holy Spirit is God's presence in our lives. He is called the Holy Spirit because He brings holiness. Holiness is the character or essence of God. Holiness is what God is like. And He comes to make us holy. The Spirit comes to bring everything in our lives under the control of God. Like a fire set within us, the Spirit is burning, molding, and moving everything within us into God's charge.

To be a Christian is to "keep in step with the Spirit" (Gal. 5:25). This will involve a crisis of purity. In following the leading of the Spirit, you will come to a point of need for a deep cleansing, a full surrender, and an inner filling of God's love. God makes your heart pure, and your heart is true to Him. The question is settled: You belong to God.

The Spirit will also lead you in a process of maturity. He seeks to deepen our understanding, refine our character, and mold our lives into the growing and enabling will of God. We live out the scripture: "Do not conform any longer to the pattern of this world, but be transformed by the renewing of your mind. Then you will be able to test and approve what God's will is—his good, pleasing, and perfect will" (Rom. 12:2).

Living Out Our Beliefs

In theological terms, God's total work of salvation includes both justification and sanctification. Put simply, God does *in us* and *for us* what we cannot do ourselves. It is our responsibility to trust and obey. In this section, we will expand on these ideas.

The diagram on the next page pictures the ideal pattern of the Christian life from its beginning to its consummation:

Justification—What Christ Does for Us

Justification means God accepts us "just-as-if" we had never sinned (Rom. 3:21-31).

- Justification begins at the moment we turn and trust Christ.
- We continue to be justified by God's grace as we permit our faith to work in love and as we walk in the light of God: Trust and obey.
- "Completed" justification will be our acquittal at the Judgment and our future home in heaven.

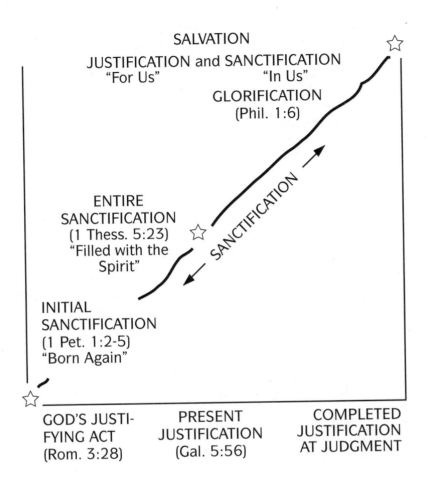

SALVATION

JUSTIFICATION and SANCTIFICATION
"For Us"   "In Us"

GLORIFICATION
(Phil. 1:6)

ENTIRE
SANCTIFICATION
(1 Thess. 5:23)
"Filled with the
Spirit"

SANCTIFICATION

INITIAL
SANCTIFICATION
(1 Pet. 1:2-5)
"Born Again"

| GOD'S JUSTI-FYING ACT (Rom. 3:28) | PRESENT JUSTIFICATION (Gal. 5:56) | COMPLETED JUSTIFICATION AT JUDGMENT |

Sanctification—What Christ Does in Us

In the broadest sense, all that God does "in us" is done by the Holy Spirit (2 Thess. 2:13; Heb. 12:14) and is called "sanctification."

- "Initial" sanctification, or the new birth, begins at the same moment as justification (1 Cor. 6:9-11; Titus 3:5-7).
- "Entire" sanctification is a distinctive moment in the process of a second stage in the work (1 Thess. 5:23-24; Rom. 6:19; Eph. 5:25-27; John 17:17).

- "Glorification" is the final perfection of sanctification toward which we are advancing as we press on in faith (Phil. 3:12-15; 1 John 3:2).

The broadest and best definition of "sanctification" is seen in the scripture, "And we, who with unveiled faces all reflect the Lord's glory, are being transformed into his likeness with ever-increasing glory, which comes from the Lord, who is the Spirit" (2 Cor. 3:18).

Let's look at the same scriptural ideas in nontechnical and nontheological terms.

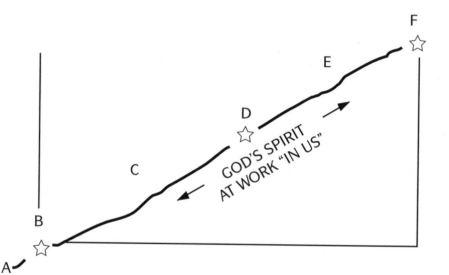

A. *The Pull of God* (sometimes called "prevenient grace," "awakening," "conscience," or "the God-shaped vacuum in every person"). This is the "pull of God" working in each individual. As people respond to it, they will discover a pathway to God in Christ.

B. *The New Beginning* (sometimes called "born again," "saved," "regenerated"). This is the result of turning from sin and trusting Jesus Christ. We are given a new beginning in life. God forgives us and comes into our lives. We have a positive Person, Jesus, to guide us.

C. *A Deepening Awareness* (sometimes called "the carnal Christian," "the immature," or "babe in Christ"). During this time of the early stages of the Christian life, we become more and more aware of our new lifestyle and the work of God in our lives. We develop in the areas of prayer, Bible study, fellowship with Christians, obedience to God, and an understanding of how He works in our lives. Day by day we grow. We turn more and more of our lives over to God.

D. *Complete Commitment and Cleansing Love* (sometimes called "entire sanctification," "the deeper walk," "the fullness of the Spirit," or "perfect love"). In our growing process, we come to a point where we turn our lives over to Jesus at a deeper and more complete level. For some, this is a time of struggle. For others, it is a natural part of their development as Christians. It is reaching the point where you know that the Bible's promise is complete in you: "May God himself, the God of peace, sanctify you through and through. May your whole spirit, soul and body be kept blameless at the coming of our Lord Jesus Christ. The one who calls you is faithful and he will do it" (1 Thess. 5:23-24).

God will cleanse your *sinful self* in perfect love. Your *natural self* is submitted to the Lordship of Jesus Christ. And your *true self* is set free in the power of the Holy Spirit.

E. *A Lifestyle of Growth* (sometimes called "Christian maturity," "growing in grace," "glory to glory"). At this stage in life, we walk in the light, even as He is in the light. We learn how to grow, how to love, and how to serve more than we ever knew before. We learn deeper lessons of humility by turning our suffering into God's glory, and we discover greater victories and the joy of serving God. We still have faults, flaws, failures, and temptations, but there is an inner certainty of faith, power, and love.

F. *Final Graduation* (sometimes called "heaven" or "glorification"). When we leave this life, we enter into life everlasting in the presence of our loving Lord. For us, death is not a wall but a door. Instant death will be instant glory.

The Place of Doctrine

Good doctrine is essential. Biblical teaching is essential. Yet we need a loving, Christlike attitude in our approach to both. In the Church of the Nazarene, there is an attitude with which we approach doctrine, theology, and Bible teaching.

A Focus on Personal Experience. Doctrine alone never saved anybody. Our trust is not in a statement of doctrine but in Jesus Christ. Only a personal relationship with Jesus Christ can truly bring God's life into our lives.

A Focus on God's Gift of Salvation. God wants our Christian lives to be balanced with all the goodness that He has given. That is why the Church of the Nazarene has its focus on God's full purpose of salvation. Saved from sin and saved to serve—this is the teaching of Scripture.

A Nondefensive Attitude. We do not have to defend God. He is big enough to defend himself. It is our job to share His love with others. This attitude gives a sense of rest as well as anticipation. We present the love of God and let His Spirit work in the people.

Godly Humility in Believers. Correct doctrine without a growing relationship with God can produce a critical attitude. When doctrine produces an attitude of superiority, there is need for deepening of the devotional life, growing in humility, and broadening of love for all others, especially those who do not agree with us.

A Doctrine That Works. John Wesley, a practical theologian, had a four-step process for working out his thinking about God. He would go to the Scripture, to church tradition, then to the test of reason, and finally he wanted something that was true to experience. Someone asked him, "What if you found a doctrine in the Bible and in church tradition that was reasonable but not true to experience?" He replied, "I would go back and see where I had misinterpreted the Bible."

A Statement of Belief

A simple statement made in the opening paragraph of this chapter is still the best statement of faith. Not only is it good doctrine, but also it is the cry of a trusting heart. It comes from Rom. 10:9: "If you confess with your mouth, 'Jesus is

Lord,' and believe in our heart that God raised him from the dead, you will be saved." This was the belief of the earliest Christians. This is the belief of Christians today. Jesus is Lord!

ARTICLES OF FAITH

I. *The Triune God*

1. We believe in one eternally existent, infinite God, Sovereign of the universe; that He only is God, creative and administrative, holy in nature, attributes, and purpose; that He, as God, is Triune in essential being, revealed as Father, Son, and Holy Spirit.

Genesis 1
Leviticus 19:2
Deuteronomy 6:4-5
Isaiah 5:16; 6:1-7; 40:18-31
Matthew 3:16-17; 28:19-20

John 14:6-27
1 Corinthians 8:6
2 Corinthians 13:14
Galatians 4:4-6
Ephesians 2:13-18

II. *Jesus Christ*

2. We believe in Jesus Christ, the Second Person of the Triune Godhead; that He was eternally one with the Father; that He became incarnate by the Holy Spirit and was born of the Virgin Mary, so that two whole and perfect natures, that is to say the Godhead and manhood, are thus united in one Person very God and very man, the God-man.

We believe that Jesus Christ died for our sins, and that He truly arose from the dead and took again His body, together with all things appertaining to the perfection of man's nature, wherewith He ascended into heaven and is there engaged in intercession for us.

Matthew 1:20-25; 16:15-16
Luke 1:26-35
John 1:1-18
Acts 2:22-36
Romans 8:3, 32-34
Galatians 4:4-5

Philippians 2:5-11
Colossians 1:12-22
1 Timothy 6:14-16
Hebrews 1:1-5;
    7:22-28, 9:24-28
1 John 1:1-3; 4:2-3, 15

III. *The Holy Spirit*

3. We believe in the Holy Spirit, the Third Person of the Triune Godhead, that He is ever present and efficiently active in and with the Church of Christ, convincing the world of sin, regenerating those who repent and believe, sanctifying believers, and guiding into all truth as it is in Jesus.

John 7:39; 14:15-18, 26;
  16:7-15
Acts 2:33; 15:8-9
Romans 8:1-27
Galatians 3:1-14; 4:6

Ephesians 3:14-21
1 Thessalonians 4:7-8
2 Thessalonians 2:13
1 Peter 1:2
1 John 3:24; 4:13

IV. *The Holy Scriptures*

4. We believe in the plenary inspiration of the Holy Scriptures, by which we understand the 66 books of the Old and New Testaments, given by divine inspiration, inerrantly revealing the will of God concerning us in all things necessary to our salvation, so that whatever is not contained therein is not to be enjoined as an article of faith.

Luke 24:44-47
John 10:35
1 Corinthians 15:3-4

2 Timothy 3:15-17
1 Peter 1:10-12
2 Peter 1:20-21

V. *Sin, Original and Personal* *

5. We believe that sin came into the world through the disobedience of our first parents, and death by sin. We believe that sin is of two kinds: original sin or depravity, and actual or personal sin.

5.1. We believe that original sin, or depravity, is that corruption of the nature of all the offspring of Adam by reason of which everyone is very far gone from original righteousness or the pure state of our first parents at the time of their creation, is averse to God, is without spiritual life, and inclined to evil, and that continually. We further believe that original sin continues to exist with the new life of the regenerate, until [eradicated] *the heart is fully cleansed* by the baptism with the Holy Spirit.

5.2. We believe that original sin differs from actual sin in that it constitutes an inherited propensity to actual sin for which no one is accountable until its divinely provided remedy is neglected or rejected.

---

*Constitutional changes adopted by the 2001 General Assembly were in the process of ratification by the district assemblies at the time of the printing of the *Manual/2001-2005*. Where changes are being made, words in italics are new words and words in brackets [ ] are words being deleted.

5.3. We believe that actual or personal sin is a voluntary violation of a known law of God by a morally responsible person. It is therefore not to be confused with involuntary and inescapable shortcomings, infirmities, faults, mistakes, failures, or other deviations from a standard of perfect conduct that are the residual effects of the Fall. However, such innocent effects do not include attitudes or responses contrary to the spirit of Christ, which may properly be called sins of the spirit. We believe that personal sin is primarily and essentially a violation of the law of love; and that in relation to Christ sin may be defined as unbelief.

Original sin

Genesis 3; 6:5
Job 15:14
Psalm 51:5
Jeremiah 17:9-10
Mark 7:21-23

Romans 1:18-25; 5:12-14;
  7:1—8:9
1 Corinthians 3:1-4
Galatians 5:16-25
1 John 1:7-8

Personal sin

Matthew 22:36-40
  (with 1 John 3:4)
John 8:34-36; 16:8-9

Romans 3:23; 6:15-23;
  8:18-24; 14:23
1 John 1:9—2:4; 3:7-10

VI. *Atonement*

6. We believe that Jesus Christ, by His sufferings, by the shedding of His own blood, and by His [meritorious] death on the Cross, made a full atonement for all human sin, and that this Atonement is the only ground of salvation, and that it is sufficient for every individual of Adam's race. The Atonement is graciously efficacious for the salvation of the irresponsible and for the children in innocency but is efficacious for the salvation of those who reach the age of responsibility only when they repent and believe.

Isaiah 53:5-6, 11
Mark 10:45
Luke 24:46-48
John 1:29; 3:14-17
Acts 4:10-12
Romans 3:21-26; 4:17-25;
  5:6-21
1 Corinthians 6:20

2 Corinthians 5:14-21
Galatians 1:3-4; 3:13-14
Colossians 1:19-23
1 Timothy 2:3-6
Titus 2:11-14
Hebrews 2:9; 9:11-14;
  13:12
1 Peter 1:18-21; 2:19-25
1 John 2:1-2

VII. *[Free Agency] Prevenient Grace*

7. We believe that the human race's creation in God-likeness included ability to choose between right and wrong, and that thus human beings were made morally responsible; that through the fall of Adam they became depraved so that they cannot now turn and prepare themselves by their own natural strength and works to faith and calling upon God. But we also believe that the grace of God through Jesus Christ is freely bestowed upon all people, enabling all who will to turn from sin to righteousness, believe on Jesus Christ for pardon and cleansing from sin, and follow good works pleasing and acceptable in His sight.

We believe that all persons, though in the possession of the experience of regeneration and entire sanctification, may fall from grace and apostatize and, unless they repent of their sins, be hopelessly and eternally lost.

Godlikeness and moral responsibility

Genesis 1:26-27; 2:16-17
Deuteronomy 28:1-2; 30:19
Joshua 24:15
Psalm 8:3-5
Isaiah 1:8-10
Jeremiah 31:29-30

Ezekiel 18:1-4
Micah 6:8
Romans 1:19-20; 2:1-16;
    14:7-12
Galatians 6:7-8

Natural inability

Job 14:4; 15:14
Psalms 14:1-4; 51:5
John 3:6*a*

Romans 3:10-12; 5:12-14,
    20*a*; 7:14-25

Free grace and works of faith

Ezekiel 18:25-26
John 1:12-13; 3:6*b*
Acts 5:31
Romans 5:6-8, 18; 6:15-16,
    23; 10:6-8; 11:22
1 Corinthians 2:9-14; 10:1-12
2 Corinthians 5:18-19
Galatians 5:6
Ephesians 2:8-10

Philippians 2:12-13
Colossians 1:21-23
2 Timothy 4:10*a*
Titus 2:11-14
Hebrews 2:1-3; 3:12-15;
    6:4-6; 10:26-31
James 2:18-22
2 Peter 1:10-11; 2:20-22

VIII. *Repentance*

8. We believe that repentance, which is a sincere and

thorough change of the mind in regard to sin, involving a sense of personal guilt and a voluntary turning away from sin, is demanded of all who have by act or purpose become sinners against God. The Spirit of God gives to all who will repent the gracious help of penitence of heart and hope of mercy, that they may believe unto pardon and spiritual life.

2 Chronicles 7:14
Psalms 32:5-6; 51:1-17
Isaiah 55:6-7
Jeremiah 3:12-14
Ezekiel 18:30-32; 33:14-16
Mark 1:14-15
Luke 3:1-14; 13:1-5;
    18:9-14

Acts 2:38; 3:19; 5:31;
    17:30-31; 26:16-18
Romans 2:4
2 Corinthians 7:8-11
1 Thessalonians 1:9
2 Peter 3:9

IX. *Justification, Regeneration, and Adoption*

9. We believe that justification is the gracious and judicial act of God by which He grants full pardon of all guilt and complete release from the penalty of sins committed, and acceptance as righteous, to all who believe on Jesus Christ and receive Him as Lord and Savior.

10. We believe that regeneration, or the new birth, is that gracious work of God whereby the moral nature of the repentant believer is spiritually quickened and given a distinctively spiritual life, capable of faith, love, and obedience.

11. We believe that adoption is that gracious act of God by which the justified and regenerated believer is constituted a son of God.

12. We believe that justification, regeneration, and adoption are simultaneous in the experience of seekers after God and are obtained upon the condition of faith, preceded by repentance; and that to this work and state of grace the Holy Spirit bears witness.

Luke 18:14
John 1:12-13; 3:3-8; 5:24
Acts 13:39
Romans 1:17; 3:21-26, 28;
    4:5-9, 17-25; 5:1, 16-
    19; 6:4; 7:6; 8:1, 15-17
1 Corinthians 1:30; 6:11

Galatians 2:16-21; 3:1-14,
    26; 4:4-7
Ephesians 1:6-7; 2:1, 4-5
Philippians 3:3-9
Colossians 2:13
Titus 3:4-7
1 Peter 1:23

39

2 Corinthians 5:17-21   1 John 1:9; 3:1-2, 9; 4:7;
                                     5:1, 9-13, 18

X. *Entire Sanctification*

13. We believe that entire sanctification is that act of God, subsequent to regeneration, by which believers are made free from original sin, or depravity, and brought into a state of entire devotement to God, and the holy obedience of love made perfect.

It is wrought by the baptism with the Holy Spirit, and comprehends in one experience the cleansing of the heart from sin and the abiding, indwelling presence of the Holy Spirit, empowering the believer for life and service.

Entire sanctification is provided by the blood of Jesus, is wrought instantaneously by faith, preceded by entire consecration; and to this work and state of grace the Holy Spirit bears witness.

This experience is also known by various terms representing its different phases, such as "Christian perfection," "perfect love," "heart purity," "the baptism with the Holy Spirit," "the fullness of the blessing," and "Christian holiness."

14. We believe that there is a marked distinction between a pure heart and a mature character. The former is obtained in an instant, the result of entire sanctification; the latter is the result of growth in grace.

We believe that the grace of entire sanctification includes the impulse to grow in grace. However, this impulse must be consciously nurtured, and careful attention given to the requisites and processes of spiritual development and improvement in Christlikeness of character and personality. Without such purposeful endeavor one's witness may be impaired and the grace itself frustrated and ultimately lost.

Jeremiah 31:31-34
Ezekiel 36:25-27
Malachi 3:2-3
Matthew 3:11-12
Luke 3:16-17
John 7:37-39; 14:15-23;
    17:6-20
Acts 1:5; 2:1-4; 15:8-9

2 Corinthians 6:14—7:1
Galatians 2:20; 5:16-25
Ephesians 3:14-21; 5:17-
    18, 25-27
Philippians 3:10-15
Colossians 3:1-17
1 Thessalonians 5:23-24
Hebrews 4:9-11; 10:10-17;

Romans 6:11-13, 19;   12:1-2; 13:12
  8:1-4, 8-14; 12:1-2   1 John 1:7, 9

"Christian perfection," "perfect love"
Deuteronomy 30:6   Philippians 3:10-15
Matthew 5:43-48; 22:37-40 Hebrews 6:1
Romans 12:9-21; 13:8-10   1 John 4:17-18
1 Corinthians 13

"Heart purity"
Matthew 5:8   1 Peter 1:22
Acts 15:8-9   1 John 3:3

"Baptism with the Holy Spirit"
Jeremiah 31:31-34   Matthew 3:11-12
Ezekiel 36:25-27   Luke 3:16-17
Malachi 3:2-3   Acts 1:5; 2:1-4; 15:8-9

"Fullness of the blessing"
Romans 15:29

"Christian holiness"

Matthew 5:1—7:29   2 Timothy 2:19-22
John 15:1-11   Hebrews 10:19-25; 12:14;
Romans 12:1—15:3   13:20-21
2 Corinthians 7:1   1 Peter 1:15-16
Ephesians 4:17—5:20   2 Peter 1:1-11; 3:18
Philippians 1:9-11; 3:12-15   Jude 20-21
Colossians 2:20—3:17
1 Thessalonians 3:13;
   4:7-8; 5:23

XI. *The Church*

15. We believe in the Church, the community that confesses Jesus Christ as Lord, the covenant people of God made new in Christ, the Body of Christ called together by the Holy Spirit through the Word.

God calls the Church to express its life in the unity and fellowship of the Spirit; in worship through the preaching of the Word, observance of the sacraments, and ministry in His name; by obedience to Christ and mutual accountability.

The mission of the Church in the world is to continue the redemptive work of Christ in the power of the Spirit through holy living, evangelism, discipleship, and service.

The Church is a historical reality, which organizes itself in culturally conditioned forms; exists both as local congregations and as a universal body; sets apart persons called of God for specific ministries. God calls the Church to live under His rule in anticipation of the consummation at the coming of our Lord Jesus Christ.

Exodus 19:3
Jeremiah 31:33
Matthew 8:11; 10:7; 16:13-19,
 24; 18:15-20; 28:19-20
John 17:14-26; 20:21-23
Acts 1:7-8; 2:32-47;
 6:1-2; 13:1; 14:23
Romans 2:28-29; 4:16; 10:9-
 15; 11:13-32; 12:1-8;
 15:1-3
1 Corinthians 3:5-9; 7:17;
 11:1, 17-33; 12:3, 12-
 31; 14:26-40

2 Corinthians 5:11—6:1
Galatians 5:6, 13-14; 6:1-
 5, 15
Ephesians 4:1-17; 5:25-27
Philippians 2:1-16
1 Thessalonians 4:1-12
1 Timothy 4:13
Hebrews 10:19-25
1 Peter 1:1-2, 13; 2:4-12,
 21; 4:1-2, 10-11
1 John 4:17
Jude 24
Revelation 5:9-10

XII. *Baptism*

16. We believe that Christian baptism, commanded by our Lord, is a sacrament signifying acceptance of the benefits of the atonement of Jesus Christ, to be administered to believers and declarative of their faith in Jesus Christ as their Savior, and full purpose of obedience in holiness and righteousness.

Baptism being a symbol of the new covenant, young children may be baptized, upon request of parents or guardians who shall give assurance for them of necessary Christian training.

Baptism may be administered by sprinkling, pouring, or immersion, according to the choice of the applicant.

Matthew 3:1-7; 28:16-20
Acts 2:37-41; 8:35-39; 10:44-
 48; 16:29-34; 19:1-6
Romans 6:3-4

Galatians 3:26-28
Colossians 2:12
1 Peter 3:18-22

XIII. *The Lord's Supper*

17. We believe that the Memorial and Communion Supper instituted by our Lord and Savior Jesus Christ is essentially a New Testament sacrament, declarative of His sacrificial death, through the merits of which believers have life and salvation and promise of all spiritual blessings in Christ. It is distinctively for those who are prepared for reverent appreciation of its significance, and by it they show forth the Lord's death till He comes again. It being the Communion feast, only those who have faith in Christ and love for the saints should be called to participate therein.

Exodus 12:1-14
Matthew 26:26-29
Mark 14:22-25
Luke 22:17-20

John 6:28-58
1 Corinthians 10:14-21;
11:23-32

XIV. *Divine Healing*

18. We believe in the Bible doctrine of divine healing and urge our people to seek to offer the prayer of faith for the healing of the sick. We also believe God heals through the means of medical science.

2 Kings 5:1-19
Psalm 103:1-5
Matthew 4:23-24; 9:18-35
John 4:46-54

Acts 5:12-16; 9:32-42;
14:8-15
1 Corinthians 12:4-11
2 Corinthians 12:7-10
James 5:13-16

XV. *Second Coming of Christ*

19. We believe that the Lord Jesus Christ will come again; that we who are alive at His coming shall not precede them that are asleep in Christ Jesus; but that, if we are abiding in Him, we shall be caught up with the risen saints to meet the Lord in the air, so that we shall ever be with the Lord.

Matthew 25:31-46
John 14:1-3
Acts 1:9-11
Philippians 3:20-21
1 Thessalonians 4:13-18

Titus 2:11-14
Hebrews 9:26-28
2 Peter 3:3-15
Revelation 1:7-8; 22:7-20

XVI. *Resurrection, Judgment, and Destiny*

20. We believe in the resurrection of the dead, that the bodies of both the just and of the unjust shall be raised to life and united with their spirits—"they that have done good, unto the resurrection of life; and they that have done evil, unto the resurrection of damnation."

21. We believe in future judgment in which every person shall appear before God to be judged according to his or her deeds in this life.

22. We believe that glorious and everlasting life is assured to all who savingly believe in, and obediently follow, Jesus Christ our Lord; and that the finally impenitent shall suffer eternally in hell.

Genesis 18:25
1 Samuel 2:10
Psalm 50:6
Isaiah 26:19
Daniel 12:2-3
Matthew 25:31-46
Mark 9:43-48
Luke 16:19-31; 20:27-38

John 3:16-18; 5:25-29;
    11:21-27
Acts 17:30-31
Romans 2:1-16; 14:7-12
1 Corinthians 15:12-58
2 Corinthians 5:10
2 Thessalonians 1:5-10
Revelation 20:11-15; 22:1-15

4

How We Are Organized

Leadership and organization are essential to a church. A grade school assignment given to an entire class was to determine the course of action they would take if stranded on a deserted island. After debating the need for food, fire, and shelter, the children quickly discovered that the first need was for leadership and organization.

Jesus understood this: "When Jesus landed and saw a large crowd, he had compassion on them, because they were like sheep without a shepherd" (Mark 6:34).

In this chapter we will look at the organization of the Church of the Nazarene. We will examine three areas: how we are organized through leadership; how we are organized financially; how we are organized for ministry.

How We Are Organized Through Leadership

Historically, there are three basic patterns of church government. The first is *episcopal*. Bishops are elected or appointed for life and make the most basic decisions. They appoint pastors. The voice of laypeople is limited in church affairs. This is found in Roman Catholic and Eastern Orthodox Churches. It is also found in the Episcopal Church, but here laypeople have a larger voice and participate in electing bishops.

The *congregational* form is used by Congregational, Baptist, and independent churches. Here, the local members or the local pastor have control. There are few ties with other churches within the denomination. There is much independence and little worldwide coordination. Denominations of this type may have a general meeting, but decisions of the general meeting are not binding on local churches.

The *presbyterian* form is representative. There are no bishops. Local churches are part of larger units (presbytery or synod) and are represented at these larger units by clergy and lay representatives. These bodies elect delegates to the general meeting. The decisions of the general meeting are binding on lower bodies, including local churches. Clergy and laypeople cooperate at every level of church government. Presbyterian and Reformed Churches are the primary churches of this type.

The Church of the Nazarene draws upon all three models, like most churches in the Wesleyan family. From the *episcopal* model it draws a concept of superintendency at the district and general levels. But district and general superintendents in the Church of the Nazarene are elected for specified terms and must be reelected to continue in office. From the *presbyterian* model, Nazarenes have adapted a system of interlocking assemblies (district assembly and general assembly). And from the *congregational* model, the denomination employs the right of local churches to call their own pastors. Lay members are represented and exert influence on each of the church's three levels: local, district, and general.

The General Church

The worldwide Church of the Nazarene is led by a board of six *general superintendents*. They are elected to four-year terms (a quadrennium). Each supervises a specific world area in our mission work. Each is assigned to certain departments in an advisory capacity. And a general superintendent will preside at each district assembly.

General superintendents are elected at the *general assembly*. This is the legislative body of the church. It is composed of clergy and lay delegates from districts around the world. Major decisions and changes in the constitution take place at the general assembly. These changes are binding on the whole church.

Much of the day-to-day business of the general church occurs at its *international Headquarters* in Kansas City, Missouri, where information and resources for districts and churches worldwide are gathered and disseminated.

The international Headquarters currently is comprised of three departments (World Mission/Evangelism, USA/Canada

Mission/Evangelism, and Sunday School Ministries) and three general offices (general secretary, general treasurer, and International Board of Education).

World Mission/Evangelism. This department oversees the church's mission outreach in many parts of the world. It supervises the work of the church's missionaries, coordinates Work and Witness teams, and oversees Nazarene Compassionate Ministries International. Nazarene Missions International, an auxiliary of the department, is a vehicle through which the local, district, and general mission support programs are promoted.

USA/Canada Mission/Evangelism. This department encompasses ministries in the United States and Canada that promote evangelism, clergy services, chaplaincy, and multicultural ministries. It promotes compassionate (or social) ministries and works with U.S. and Canadian district superintendents to develop mission strategies.

Sunday School Ministries. This department is responsible for producing curriculum for all ages—children, youth, adults, and senior adults. It is also responsible for Continuing Lay Training, and it produces a wide variety of other discipleship resources.

General secretary. Legal and corporate matters of the international Church of the Nazarene are handled by the general secretary/Headquarters operations officer. This office maintains ministerial records, statistics, and the Nazarene Archives. It is responsible for church relations and news services. And it serves all Headquarters in the areas of personnel, business services, and current technologies.

General treasurer. The general treasurer/Headquarters financial officer is responsible for receiving funds for general interests and disbursing them as directed by the General Board. It administers the General Church Loan Fund, which makes loans available for new churches. It promotes stewardship in the local church, and it channels funds donated to church causes via wills, trusts, annuities, and investments through the Office of Planned Giving.

International Board of Education. Led by a commissioner of education, this board links with the Nazarene institutions around the world that offer postsecondary education (education beyond the high school level). It strives to equip schools in any area where they need assistance, including finances. It facilitates faculty and theology conferences and seeks ways for teachers at Nazarene schools in the developed nations to assist those in less affluent world areas.

The District Church

The Church of the Nazarene is divided into *districts* around the world.

A district is led by a *district superintendent,* who supervises the establishing of new churches, the calling of pastors, and the coordinating of district activities, and gives spiritual guidance and encouragement. On Phase 3 districts,* the district superintendent is elected at the *district assembly.* Elected representatives from all churches meet once a year to hear reports from the district superintendent, pastors, and district ministries.

During the year, the *District Advisory Board,* made up of an equal number of laity and clergy, meets with the district superintendent to coordinate the activities of the district. Advisory Board members are elected by the district assembly. A partial list of the purpose of the district church would include:

- The examination and encouragement of people who seek service as full-time Christian ministers (known as the District Ministerial Credentials Board)
- The planting of new churches and ministries as well as the financial and spiritual support of small churches and ministries that cannot support themselves (known as the District Home Missions Board)
- The examination and approval or disapproval of propositions submitted by local churches concerning building, the purchase of property, and indebtedness (known as the District Church Properties Board)
- The encouragement of growth of local churches in the area of Sunday School (known as the District Sunday School Ministries Board)
- The coordination of the activities for young people in our churches (known as the District Nazarene Youth International) as well as children's and adult ministries
- The informing, inspiring, and involvement of people in a

---

*One hundred percent self-supporting in district administration.

vision for world missions (known as the District Nazarene Missions International)

The Local Church

The spiritual leader of the local church is the *pastor*. He
or she is elected by the people and periodically presented to
the church board in cooperation with the district superintendent for review and evaluation. The pastor is then affirmed by
the board or presented to the congregation for reelection.

The task of the pastor is twofold:

- *Administration,* including *(a)* representing the district
  and general church, *(b)* chairman of the church board,
  and *(c)* coordinating the church program
- *Ministry,* including *(a)* preaching the Word, *(b)* building
  up believers in the faith, and *(c)* caring for the spiritual
  needs of the church

The major assignment of the pastor is to be the spiritual
leader of the church. As the Scripture instructs:

> To the elders among you, I appeal as a fellow elder, a
> witness of Christ's sufferings and one who also will share
> in the glory to be revealed: Be shepherds of God's flock
> that is under your care, serving as overseers—not be-
> cause you must, but because you are willing, as God
> wants you to be; not greedy for money, but eager to
> serve; not lording it over those entrusted to you, but be-
> ing examples to the flock. And when the Chief Shepherd
> appears, you will receive the crown of glory that will never
> fade away *(1 Pet. 5:1-4).*

Many churches have *associate ministers.* These individuals are nominated by the pastor, approved by the district superintendent, and elected by the church board. Their duties
are supervised by the pastor.

The *church board* is the official decision-making body of
the church. Those serving on the church board are elected by
the members each year. These people are (1) spiritual leaders
in setting the tone of the church in terms of prayer, faith, love,
and joy; (2) church growth leaders as they envision expansion,
evangelism, and outreach; and (3) financial leaders in the coordinating and careful use of all church programs, resources,
and funds.

The pastor, associate ministers, and church board members are to strive for excellence concerning the biblical requirements for church leadership. These requirements are found in 1 Tim. 3:1-13 and Titus 1:5-9. These are outlined in the supplement at the end of this chapter titled "Church Leadership."

The *Sunday School Ministries Board* consists of the chairperson and representatives of the congregation elected by the members. Their primary responsibility is overseeing and encouraging growth in the Sunday School. They also supervise programs involving the nursery, children, youth, and adults.

The *members* of the church are the "official" church body and family. As members, we take responsibility for "being the church" and "doing the ministry of the church."

All members age 15 and older vote on: (1) the call of the pastor; (2) the election of church officers including the church board, chairperson of the Sunday School Ministries Board, missionary president, Nazarene Youth International president, and representatives to the district assembly; and (3) the purchase and sale of all property and buildings.

More important than these official duties, members are involved in supporting the local church financially, participating in the ministry of the local church, and serving Jesus Christ through this body of believers. The words shared with the congregation at the time of the reception of new members are:

Dearly Beloved: The privileges and blessings that we have in association together in the Church of Jesus Christ are very sacred and precious. There is in it such hallowed fellowship as cannot otherwise be known.

There is such helpfulness with brotherly watch care and counsel as can be found only in the Church

There is the godly care of pastors, with the teachings of the Word; and the helpful inspiration of social worship. And there is cooperation in service, accomplishing that which cannot otherwise be done. The doctrines upon which the church rests as essential to Christian experience are brief.

We believe in God the Father, Son, and Holy Spirit. We especially emphasize the deity of Jesus Christ and the personality of the Holy Spirit.

We believe that human beings are born in sin; that

they need the work of forgiveness through Christ and the new birth by the Holy Spirit; that subsequent to this there is the deeper work of heart cleansing or entire sanctification through the infilling of the Holy Spirit, and that to each of these works of grace the Holy Spirit gives witness.

We believe that our Lord will return, the dead shall be raised, and that all shall come to final judgment with its rewards and punishments.

Do you heartily believe these truths? If so, answer, "I do."

Do you acknowledge Jesus Christ as your personal Savior, and do you realize that He saves you now?

Response: I do.

Desiring to unite with the Church of the Nazarene, do you covenant to give yourself to the fellowship and work of God in connection with it, as set forth in the General Rules and the Covenant of Christian Conduct of the Church of the Nazarene? Will you endeavor in every way to glorify God, by a humble walk, godly conversation, and holy service; by devotedly giving of your means; by faithful attendance upon the means of grace; and, abstaining from all evil, will you seek earnestly to perfect holiness of heart and life in the fear of the Lord?

Response: I will.

I welcome you into this church, to its sacred fellowship, responsibilities, and privileges. May the great Head of the Church bless and keep you, and enable you to be faithful in all good works, that your life and witness may be effective in leading others to Christ.

The Attitude of Unity

It is possible to have the best organization and the best leadership with no progress for the kingdom of Christ. The leadership, organization, and membership of the local church must be infused with the proper spiritual attitude. It is the attitude of *Unity.*

As a prisoner for the Lord, then, I urge you to live a life worthy of the calling you have received. Be completely humble and gentle; be patient, bearing with one another in love. Make every effort to *keep the unity of the Spirit* through the bond of peace. There is one body and one Spirit . . . one hope . . . one Lord, one faith, one baptism; one God and Father of all, who is over all and through all and in all *(Eph. 4:1-6, italics added).*

How We Are Organized Financially

We believe in a positive approach to the church and its financial needs. We do not believe in simply "giving to the church." We believe in giving to the glory of God: "This service that you perform is not only supplying the needs of God's people but is also overflowing in many expressions of thanks to God. Because of the service by which you have proved yourselves, men will praise God for the obedience that accompanies your confession of the gospel of Christ, and for your generosity in sharing with them and with everyone else" (2 Cor. 9:12-13).

What the Money Is For

There is a three-step process involved in determining the expenditures of the church. Let us outline these steps:

Needs of the People. We begin with the question "What do we need?" We do not ignore the question "What can we afford?" but we believe that if the need is great, God will supply the resources in His time and in His way, through His people.

The Budget. The budget represents the financial support necessary to meet the needs of the congregation through the ministries of the church. The budget, approved by the church board, takes into account:

- Giving to Others (approximately 20-25 percent of the budget*). This includes World Missions (World Evangelism Fund), Nazarene higher education, district support, retired ministers and missionaries pension fund, and local community action.
- Local Ministries (approximately 50-60 percent of the budget). This includes support of all church programs, the pastor, the staff, and ministries to people.

---

*Approximations represent averages of most churches.

- The Building and Property (approximately 20-25 percent of the budget). This includes debt reduction, utilities, maintenance, and plans for expansion.

Our Faith. Financial needs are presented to the congregation. In faith, as each member is obedient to God, we believe the need will be met. Jesus is Lord of all in the church. He is also the Lord of our finance.

Where the Money Comes From

There are three sources of income for most local churches. They are:

- Special Events. Occasionally, a special dinner, retreat, outing, or group activity will involve a minimum charge.
- Special Offerings. These would include (1) gifts to world missions; (2) gifts toward special projects, furnishings, and other special items not included in the budget; and (3) church building fund or improvement projects.
- Consistent Giving. The majority of our financial support comes from consistent giving. We expect and need to be consistent givers. We are a tithing church. A tithe is 10 percent of your earnings. We tithe for three reasons: *duty*—Jesus told us not to neglect the tithe (Matt. 23:23); *blessing*—our God blesses spiritually (Mal. 3:10); *love*—this is the deepest and oldest motivation for tithing (Gen. 14:20).

Let us invite you and your family to pray and consider the possibilities of consistent giving. May God guide you and encourage you in this important spiritual decision. To learn more about tithing, read the material at the end of this chapter titled "Having the Tithe of Your Life."

This is a *personal decision.* You must follow God's leading in your life. The Bible is convincing: "Each man should give what he has decided in his heart to give, not reluctantly or under compulsion, for God loves a cheerful giver" (2 Cor. 9:7).

How We Are Organized for Ministry

It is wonderful to have leadership and organization based upon God's will spoken through His Word and His people. It is wonderful to have the financial structure of the church built upon the needs of the congregation and the dedication of

God's people to meet the needs through faith. Yet these are simply supports to the true function of the church:

- We are here for *ministry,* not government and leadership.
- We are here for *ministry,* not finances or budgets.
- We are here for *ministry,* not organization and structure.

The following are three functions of ministry that we want to keep in balance:

The "Hook" of Evangelism

Jesus called fishermen to be "fishers of men" (Matt. 4:19; Mark 1:17). He taught them how to win others into the kingdom of God. This is known as evangelism.

We are reaching into the homes and lives of people who are unchurched. Not many of the songs, rituals, and words that we use in church are familiar to them. It is our duty to be servants of God in introducing people to His kingdom. Therefore we work on this premise: *The needs of the unchurched must be kept in focus when planning the church program.*

Evangelism is limited only by our imagination. Some of the things we do include

- Special classes and seminars are advertised through the community that will meet the needs of people who are not attending church.
- Many of the pastor's messages are designed for those who are unfamiliar with the church and Scripture, to bring them into a personal relationship with Christ.
- Occasionally we will have special events or guests to attract unchurched people.
- We have special services and revivals to which we invite neighbors, family, and friends to hear the message of Jesus Christ and His love.
- God calls some within the church family to be "evangelists" on an individual or small-group basis. They work with friends, neighbors, and family on a one-to-one basis or in Bible studies in their homes.

Evangelism is building a bridge of love so that we might earn the right to share the good news of Jesus Christ with them.

The "Book" of Education

The "Book" we refer to is the Bible. It is not enough to introduce people to the love of God; we must teach a Bible-based lifestyle. This is the process of Christian education. Our Christian education program is built on this premise: *The Holy Spirit is the greatest Teacher of all. He is the guiding Force in training people to live productive and positive Christian lives.* There are several avenues of Christian education in the church:

- During the Sunday School hour, we offer classes for every age-group and interest, each focusing on different aspects and truths of Christian living and Bible understanding from the Wesleyan perspective.
- Often the pastor's sermon is designed to help one grow spiritually through the great truths and passages of Scripture.
- The midweek evening Bible study is an in-depth look at various topics of interest and concern for growing Christians.
- Occasionally we will have special events, seminars, or classes that are designed to enrich the lives of Christians.
- You will discover that the church is filled with mature Christians who can help in your spiritual growth. Many of them are willing to counsel, teach, and share the great wisdom of God in their lives.

The "Crook" of Caring Ministries

In Bible times, the "crook" was the tool of the shepherd. It was through this instrument that he would care for and tend the sheep. It is this process of caring that develops positive and loving relationships in the church. The best expression of this in the New Testament is "family." The caring and relationship ministries of our church are based on the premise: *We desire to develop a positive, loving, family atmosphere in which people can live and grow in the love of God.* There are several ways in which we try to develop caring relationships:

- We encourage our people to open their homes to one another in the ministry of hospitality.
- Some individuals set aside time every week to call on new members, guests, friends of the church, shut-ins,

the sick, the elderly, or those in crisis and need.

- Many churches have a benevolence fund, administered by a stewardship committee designed to help in times of crisis and tragedy.
- We encourage our Sunday School classes and the church as a whole to be involved in times of fellowship, church dinners, and activities, knowing that positive relationships can be built in which the love of Christ is shared.
- We also realize that true concern is "caught rather than taught." It is a spontaneous expression of love prompted by God's presence within.

A Place to Begin

As you become a member, it will help you if you become involved in the ministry of the church in several ways:

- We encourage you to ask God to help you share the Good News, individually or through the church, with three people in the next three months.
- We encourage you to begin a daily time of Bible study and prayer.
- We invite you to get involved in one of the small groups in the church through the Sunday School, Bible study, weeknight programs, and so on.
- Also, we invite you to find a place of service in one of the many areas of ministry in the church.

A Philosophy of Ministry

A philosophy of ministry is exemplified in the following passage of Scripture:

It was he who gave some to be apostles, some to be prophets, some to be evangelists, and some to be pastors and teachers, to prepare God's people for works of service, so that the body of Christ may be built up until we all reach unity in the faith and in the knowledge of the Son of God and become mature, attaining to the whole measure of the fullness of Christ. Then we will no longer be infants, tossed back and forth by the waves, and blown here and there by every wind of teaching and by the cunning and craftiness of men in their deceitful scheming. Instead, speaking the truth in love, we will in all things grow up into him who is the Head, that is, Christ. From him the whole body, joined and held together by every supporting ligament, grows and builds itself up in love, as each part does its work *(Eph. 4:11-16)*.

This is the glory of the church. Everyone is involved. Everyone is a minister. *There is a place for you* in the government, leadership, and organization of the church. *There is a place for you* in the faithful financial support of the church. *There is a place for you* in the ministry and outreach of the church

Supplementary Information

Church Leadership

Bishops and *elders* are words that are used in the New Testament for areas of responsibility in church life. We see this in these passages (most KJV):

Acts 20:28 (ASV)	Acts 20:17
1 Tim. 3:1-2	1 Tim. 5:17, 19
Titus 1:7	Titus 1:5

Bishop is one who oversees. *Elder* is a Jewish word for a leader in the community. Our concern is not with a title but with a trust. It is the nurture and spiritual well-being of the church that is handed over to a group of people for care. It is a responsibility and a mission.

Qualifications of Leaders

Thou Shalt Nots
Be overbearing (Titus 1:7)
Be quick-tempered (Titus 1:7)
Be given to wine (1 Tim. 3:3; Titus 1:7, both KJV)
Be violent (1 Tim. 3:3; Titus 1:7)
Be quarrelsome (1 Tim. 3:3)
Be greedy, dishonest, or a lover of money (1 Tim. 3:3; Titus 1:7; 1 Pet. 5:2)
Be a new convert (1 Tim. 3:6)

Positive Qualifications
Be above reproach (1 Tim. 3:2; Titus 1:6-7)
Be the husband of one wife (1 Tim. 3:2; Titus 1:6)
Be temperate and self-controlled (1 Tim. 3:2; Titus 1:8)

Be respectable (1 Tim. 3:2)
Be hospitable (Tim. 3:2; Titus 1:8)
Be able to teach (1 Tim. 3:2)
Be a good manager of home and family (1 Tim. 3:4; Titus 1:6)
Be respected outside the church (1 Tim. 3:7)
Be upright, holy, disciplined, a lover of good (Titus 1:8)
Be solid in God's Word (Titus 1:9)

Leadership Tasks

Shepherd the flock of God (Acts 20:28; 1 Tim. 3:5; 1 Pet. 5:2)
Be an example to the flock (1 Pet. 5:3)
Teach and exhort (1 Tim. 3:2; Titus 1:9)
Gently refute those who contradict the truth (2 Tim. 2:24-26; Titus 1:9, 11)
Manage the church of God (1 Tim. 3:5)

Direction

In looking at leadership in the church, the <u>first</u> emphasis is on the qualifications. We must remember that the person is more important than the procedure. Also, tasks change but qualifications don't. Mature character results in quality leadership. <u>Second</u>, the goal of our leaders is maturity, the fullness of Christ (Eph. 4:11-13). They lead in *faith,* confidence in Jesus Christ; *hope,* stability in God's Word; and *love,* service and fellowship in God's family. The way to be a spiritual leader is through the Spirit of God.

Having the Tithe of Your Life

Your greatest opportunities are not found primarily in the circumstances that surround you but in the spiritual condition within you. Tithing is a tremendous opportunity for you to grow as a Christian in your commitment to Christ, in the blessings He has for you, and in your obedience as a true disciple. Yet the opportunity of tithing is not simply a matter of the size of the gift, but rather an attitude in the heart.

The tithe is 10 percent of your earnings given to the work of your local church. Yet in the broad and deep scriptural context, the tithe is an expression of the condition of your heart.

Wishing to test this theory, one new church began a program that would enlist everyone in tithing. They had three rules:

1. Everyone shall give.
2. Everyone shall give a tithe.
3. Everyone shall give a tithe cheerfully.

One man with a very large income wrote out a small check and placed it on the treasurer's desk. The treasurer responded, "Sir, you have fulfilled the first rule, but not the second. I cannot accept your gift." Understandably, the church member became rather distraught.

After watching the other people give their full tithe, this wealthy man returned to the desk, grudgingly wrote out his tithe check, and threw it on the ledger, saying, "Here is my tithe."

Again, the treasurer responded, "Sir, you have fulfilled the first two rules, but not the third. I cannot accept your gift."

We may have little confidence in this group's procedure for collecting the gifts of the people. However, we can have great confidence in their understanding of the depth and meaning of the tithe.

Tithing is not grudgingly giving 10 percent to God's work and selfishly hoarding the other 90 percent for your own pleasure and design. Somewhere we have been taught that the tithe marks the difference between God's money and our money. Nothing could be further from the truth. When we come to Christ in full commitment, we give Him past, present, future, family, successes, failures, and *all* of our material possessions. As Christians, all of our money belongs to God. The tithe is a natural expression of praise given from a heart of love, obedience, and blessing.

If the heart is right, tithing is a great joy and celebration. We remember one church that would break into applause and shouts of "Amen" when it was announced that it was time for the "morning tithes and offerings." However, if the heart is wrong, tithing is a mockery, a sham, and a spiritual slap in the face to our loving Lord and Savior.

This is the meaning of Jesus when He said: "Woe to you, teachers of the law and Pharisees, you hypocrites! You give a tenth of your spices—mint, dill and cummin. But you have neglected the more important matters of the law—justice, mercy and faithfulness. You should have practiced the latter, without neglecting the former. You blind guides! You strain out a gnat but swallow a camel" (Matt. 23:23-24).

In the days of Christ, there were some Pharisees and teachers of the law that would use the ritual of tithing as a screen for a heart of selfishness. They were so ritualistic about tithing that they would count the small herbs from the garden in their own home to be sure that they were tithing on all they had, yet they missed the inner nature of justice, mercy, and faithfulness.

They would tithe on the mint leaves that they raised for their families and ignore the injustice that was going on around them. They would tithe on the dill seeds and overlook people in real need. They would tithe on their cumin (an aromatic herb), yet their hearts did not produce a pleasant spiritual odor of faithfulness. In fact, they were unfaithful in their deep relationship with God.

Jesus summarized their condition by saying they would "strain out a gnat but swallow a camel." In the law of the Pharisees a gnat and a camel were considered "unclean" and not to be consumed. The picture He draws is of someone who will strain out a gnat from his cup and then fill his place with camel meat. In other words, they would fulfill the smallest ritual of the law and lose the relationship that the law was intended to establish.

Jesus did not come to do away with tithing. Rather, He came to lift tithing to its highest spiritual realm. For a Christian, it is not enough simply to tithe. We must tithe from a heart that is right with God. This opens the doors of opportunity through tithing.

What kind of a heart do we need in order to tithe the way Jesus would have us? The Scripture teaches three qualities of heart for tithing.

Tithe from a heart of blessing. God has blessed us in the past, in the present, and He will bless us in the future. We have received from God, and we know we will receive again. This is a strong motivation in tithing.

We are uncomfortable with those who "guarantee" that if we give God $10, He will give $100 in return. Some of the blessings that God gives us are better than money. He may want to give you children who have accepted Jesus as their Savior. He may want to give you the joy of seeing a missionary project grow to fruition. He may want to give you the excitement of seeing those in need come to a place of abundance in Christ. He may want to give you the thrill of participating in the growth of your church.

However, there are many times when God blesses financially. There are the "mailbox miracles" of unexpected income. There are the items we purchase on sale when we needed them and did not expect to find a sale. And there is the wisdom of the Holy Spirit in helping us use and manage our money wisely.

One man of God reminds his friends, "When I am struggling financially, I know it is time to give more." He has discovered the blessings of tithing.

Tithe from a heart of obedience. Tithing is God's way outlined in His Word. The greatest moment of tithing in the Old Testament came when the people gave obediently from hearts of love and joy: "The Israelites generously gave . . . They brought a great amount, a tithe of everything . . . of their herds and flocks and a tithe of the holy things dedicated to the LORD their God, and they piled them in heaps. . . . They praised the LORD and blessed his people Israel" (2 Chron. 31:5-6, 8).

Occasionally we run into someone who says, "I do not have to tithe because I am not under law but under grace." This is true, but only half true. And half-truths are the most dangerous. For example, let's take the case of Paul. He was a tither because he was a Pharisee. Then, on the way to Damascus, he was met with the presence of Jesus Christ. His rebellion was broken, he was set free from bondage and sin, and he was given the task of sharing the message of the gospel with the entire world. Now, after receiving all of these blessings from God, it is impossible to imagine that he said, "Lord, I am going to stop tithing now."

On the contrary, Paul probably went beyond his tithe. He may well have double-tithed, triple-tithed, and on occasion given 90 percent and lived on the 10 percent.

When we tithe as Christians, we obey our loving Heavenly Father. Many of us have stopped obeying our earthly fathers out of law and have begun to obey them from a deeper motivation of love. We obey them, not because they would stop loving us if we disobeyed, but because we have discovered that they are usually right. They only ask us to do what we need to do. Our Heavenly Father asks us to tithe because He knows we need to tithe. Law comes from a "fear of disobedience." Grace is seen as a "love that compels us to obey."

Tithe from a heart of love. This is the first motive in tithing; this is the deepest motive in tithing; and this is still the best motive in tithing.

The first person to tithe was Abraham (Gen. 14:20). No law had been written concerning tithing. There was no command to do so. Abraham had received a great physical victory in battle; he desired to give one-tenth of his earnings to the work of God. His tithing came from a motive of love.

Jacob, the grandson of Abraham, also learned to tithe from a motive of love (Gen. 28:22). After winning a great spiritual victory in which he saw the windows of heaven open and the promise of God before him, Jacob made a vow to tithe 10 percent of all that he earned. His tithing came from a motive of love.

The appeal of Jesus is to go back to the original motive of tithing: loving obedience to a God who blesses us. Jesus tells us not to neglect the tithe but to tithe from a right motive.

Tithing is written into the very nature of human beings. God does not create a law simply because He is looking for something to do. He wrote the law against stealing because He had built that law into our hearts at the time of creation. He wrote the law against adultery because God understands the nature of the marriage relationship. And God instructs us to tithe because He understands the relationship that we have with our loving Heavenly Father. Tithing is a natural response to a loving God. It is written into our own nature.

A Practical Example. His name was John. A pastor had the privilege of leading him to the Lord in his own living room. God saved his marriage. He watched his teenage girls become involved in the church. He attended regularly. In very dramatic ways his life turned around.

Some weeks after his conversion, he called the pastor aside and said, "Pastor, there is something I want to show you. Look at my checkbook." The pastor was not accustomed to looking into people's checkbooks or giving records. However, because the new convert invited him and wanted to share this piece of information, the pastor was willing to oblige him. There, in his checkbook, the pastor saw a check for $28.54 made out to the church.

He gave the pastor the explanation: "Each week when I am paid on Monday, I take my check to the bank. It is then that I write my tithe check to the church. I am afraid that if I wait until the end of the week, I will spend it all; so I write the check at the first of the week and carry it with me every day. It is a reminder of all God has done for me. And it tells me how much I love God."

This is the essence of tithing. From a heart that is right, the tithe becomes a glorious praise to a loving Heavenly Father whom we wish to obey because He blesses our lives.

5

How We Live as Christians

In the play *Murder in the Cathedral*, T. S. Eliot has written these lines:

> *The last temptation is the greatest treason;*
> *To do the right deed for the wrong reason.*
>
> (Part 1)

For God's people it is never good enough to be good. We must learn to be good for the right reason. Jesus shocked the spiritual world of His day with this statement: "Unless your righteousness surpasses that of the Pharisees and the teachers of the law, you will certainly not enter the kingdom of heaven" (Matt. 5:20).

To be a follower of Jesus is to obey Him in all things. Yet the motive under the obedience is the greater and deeper righteousness. Jesus said it this way: "If you *love me,* you will obey what I command" (John 14:15, italics added).

God does not simply want us to do what He says, but He wants us to *desire* to do what He says. Thus the discipline of the Christian life is first and foundationally not an allegiance to the right code, the right laws, the right set of standards, or even the right understanding of Scripture. First and foundationally, a Christian has allegiance to Christ.

Building on the Right Foundation

Christians are called to be living reminders of the presence of Christ in the world. The biblical word for this is "righteousness." The word means "conforming through grace to the image of God in childlike innocence and simplicity. It is a positive inclination to goodness which is more than just outward, although inward righteousness manifests itself outwardly" (*Beacon Dictionary of Theology,* 460).

For many people the problem of "living righteously" is a problem of floors and ceilings. We ask for the minimum and turn it into the maximum. We want to know the floor and decide to make it a ceiling.

This is done in schools. Students receive assignments and do only what is required. Rarely do we find a student who says, "I would like to write one more paper." They find the floor (minimum requirement) and make it a ceiling.

This attitude is carried into the job market. It is the approach to work that says, "What is the least amount of work I can do and still get paid?" Tragedy strikes when this is carried into the home and marriage relationship. People begin living on the edge, doing the minimum.

This negative principle is seen in the spiritual realm when the questions are asked, "Can I do such and such and still go to heaven?" "Can I do this or that and still be a Christian?" These are difficult questions to answer because they are the wrong questions to ask. The heart is still centered on self, on what "Can *I* do . . . ?"

True righteousness does not begin with what we do "for God" but with what God has done "for us" in Christ. The right foundation comes when you ask God, through the cleansing power of His Holy Spirit, to remove from your inner being all the floors and ceilings and fill the empty space with one, deep, supreme desire: to be like Jesus. Thus right living comes only from a right relationship with Christ. It is not what we do "for Christ" but "in Christ" that is the sure pattern of our lives.

Hardy C. Powers, general superintendent, said: "No amount of external safeguards can really protect us, but the love of Christ continually shed abroad in our hearts by the Holy Spirit will keep our hearts pure, our lives transparent, and our hands clean from all evil."

A Positive Attitude Toward Discipline

The Church of the Nazarene has developed three General Rules to give guidance in applying Christ's love in our hearts to the practical situations of daily living. The *Manual of the Church of the Nazarene* states:

To be identified with the visible Church is the blessed privilege and sacred duty of all who are saved from their sins and are seeking completeness in Christ Jesus. It is required of all who desire to unite with the Church of the Nazarene, and thus to walk in fellowship with us, that they shall show evidence of salvation from their sins by a godly walk and vital piety; and that they shall be, or earnestly desire to be, cleansed from all indwelling sin. They shall evidence their commitment to God—

FIRST. By doing that which is enjoined in the Word of God, which is our rule of both faith and practice, including:

(1) Loving God with all the heart, soul, mind, and strength, and one's neighbor as oneself (Exodus 20:3-6; Leviticus 19:17-18; Deuteronomy 5:7-10; 6:4-5; Mark 12:28-31; Romans 13:8-10).

(2) Pressing upon the attention of the unsaved the claims of the gospel, inviting them to the house of the Lord, and trying to compass their salvation (Matthew 28:19-20; Acts 1:8; Romans 1:14-16; 2 Corinthians 5:18-20).

(3) Being courteous to all men (Ephesians 4:32; Titus 3:2; 1 Peter 2:17; 1 John 3:18).

(4) Being helpful to those who are also of the faith, in love forbearing one another (Romans 12:13; Galatians 6:2, 10; Colossians 3:12-14).

(5) Seeking to do good to the bodies and souls of men; feeding the hungry, clothing the naked, visiting the sick and imprisoned, and ministering to the needy, as opportunity and ability are given (Matthew 25:35-36; 2 Corinthians 9:8-10; Galatians 2:10; James 2:15-16; 1 John 3:17-18).

(6) Contributing to the support of the ministry and the church and its work in tithes and offerings (Malachi 3:10; Luke 6:38; 1 Corinthians 9:14; 16:2; 2 Corinthians 9:6-10; Philippians 4:15-19).

(7) Attending faithfully all the ordinances of God, and the means of grace, including the public worship of God (Hebrews 10:25), the ministry of the Word (Acts 2:42),

the sacrament of the Lord's Supper (1 Corinthians 11:23-30); searching the Scriptures and meditating thereon (Acts 17:11; 2 Timothy 2:15; 3:14-16); family and private devotions (Deuteronomy 6:6-7; Matthew 6:6).

SECOND. By avoiding evil of every kind, including:

(1) Taking the name of God in vain (Exodus 20:7; Leviticus 19:12; James 5:12).

(2) Profaning the Lord's Day by participation in unnecessary secular activities, thereby indulging in practices that deny its sanctity (Exodus 20:8-11; Isaiah 58:13-14; Mark 2:27-28; Acts 20:7; Revelation 1:10).

(3) Sexual immorality, such as premarital or extramarital relations, perversion in any form, or looseness and impropriety of conduct (Exodus 20:14; Matthew 5:27-32; 1 Corinthians 6:9-11; Galatians 5:19; 1 Thessalonians 4:3-7).

(4) Habits or practices known to be destructive of physical and mental well-being. Christians are to regard themselves as temples of the Holy Spirit (Proverbs 20:1; 23:1-3; 1 Corinthians 6:17-20; 2 Corinthians 7:1; Ephesians 5:18).

(5) Quarreling, returning evil for evil, gossiping, slandering, spreading surmises injurious to the good names of others (2 Corinthians 12:20; Galatians 5:15; Ephesians 4:30-32; James 3:5-18; 1 Peter 3:9-10).

(6) Dishonesty, taking advantage in buying and selling, bearing false witness, and like works of darkness (Leviticus 19:10-11; Romans 12:17; 1 Corinthians 6:7-10).

(7) The indulging of pride in dress or behavior. Our people are to dress with the Christian simplicity and modesty that become holiness (Proverbs 29:23; 1 Timothy 2:8-10; James 4:6; 1 Peter 3:3-4; 1 John 2:15-17).

(8) Music, literature, and entertainments that dishonor God (1 Corinthians 10:31; 2 Corinthians 6:14-17; James 4:4).

THIRD. By abiding in hearty fellowship with the church, not inveighing against but wholly committed to its doctrines and usages and actively involved in its continuing witness and outreach (Ephesians 2:18-22; 4:1-3, 11-16; Philippians 2:1-8; 1 Peter 2:9-10).

As we learned in chapter 2, one of the characteristics of the early Church of the Nazarene was "The discipline . . . was dependent primarily upon the work of the Holy Spirit." This is still true. The intent of these three General Rules or principles is to help people find the power and guidance of the Holy Spirit in their lives on a day-to-day basis. To restate the principles:

Experience everything that is positive. We need to fill our lives with love for God and others as we share the good news of God's love with them. We need to care for the whole person, to support God's family, and to continue to mature in Jesus Christ. In short, we are to fill our lives with the good things of God.

Lay aside everything that is negative. If something is negative, evil, discouraging, or defeating to a Christian, we should not participate in it. We need to protect the worship and honor of God in our lives, our families, our witness to others, and our spiritual growth. Many attitudes and practices that are part of our culture can be destructive and hurtful to the Christian. We can get along without these things.

The bottom line is relationships. The genuine friendship and family atmosphere in the church are more important than personal habits and pleasures. Over and over in the New Testament we are encouraged to "love one another" (John 13:34-35; 15:12, 17; Rom. 12:10; 13:8; Gal. 5:13; Eph. 1:15; 4:2; Phil. 1:9; Col. 1:4; 1 Thess. 1:3; 3:12; 4:9-10; 2 Thess. 1:3; Heb. 10:24; 1 Pet. 1:22; 2:17; 3:8; 4:8; 1 John 3:11, 14, 23; 4:11-12, 20-21; 2 John 5). The Bible states, "'Everything is permissible'—but not everything is constructive. Nobody should seek his own good, but the good of others. . . . Do not cause anyone to stumble" (1 Cor. 10:23-24, 32). We place a high priority on our relationship with others in God's family.

These three General Rules are summarized in Scripture: "Run from anything that gives you . . . evil thoughts . . . but stay close to anything that makes you want to do right. Have faith and love, and enjoy the companionship of those who love the Lord and have pure hearts" (2 Tim. 2:22, TLB).

A Social Stand Through Discipline

The Holy Spirit is the great Guide in righteous living. Love for Christ is expressed in a desire to do His will. And His will is expressed in the Scriptures. There are times when the church body must stand together on certain social issues. There are times when years of mature experience have produced helpful guidelines concerning a Christlike lifestyle. The Church of the Nazarene deals with social issues and lifestyle questions in the Covenant of Christian Conduct. For the sake of discussion, these will be divided into two sections: (1) Social Issues; and (2) Guidelines and Helps.

Social Issues of the Day

Because of the attitudes and vast changes that have been taking place in our culture, it is important for the church to understand how timeless biblical principles relate to contemporary society.

Marriage and Divorce. Our first guiding principle is that the Christian marriage and family must be protected in our society. We follow two principles: commitment and compassion.

We believe that marriage is a lifelong *commitment* (Gen. 1:26-28, 31; 2:21-24; Mal. 2:13-16; Matt. 19:3-9; John 2:1-11; Eph. 5:21—6:4; 1 Thess. 4:3-8, TLB; Heb. 13:4). To encourage the lifelong commitment of marriage in accordance with the Scripture, we:

- Instruct the unmarried to abstain from premarital sex.
- Provide positive and encouraging counseling for those who are planning to be married.
- Encourage Christian marriages to develop, mature, and grow.
- Seek to save the home and marriage through the power of prayer, good counsel, and God's Holy Spirit during times of marital unhappiness.

Our second guiding principle is *compassion.* We realize that many have been deeply hurt by divorce. We want to have the compassion of Christ in ministering to the needs and healing of pain of those who have been involved in the dissolution of a marriage.

Jesus spoke to the issue of divorce (Matt. 5:31-32; 19:3-9), and we must speak with the same empathy, love, and understanding of Jesus. He died on the Cross for all people.

As such persons approach remarriage, we seek to give guidance, wisdom, and help in this important step. Remarriage should only be approached on a Christian basis with an understanding of the sanctity of the home.

Abortion. We oppose induced abortion for personal convenience or population control. We believe induced abortion to be permissible only on the basis of sound medical reasons that give evidence of life-endangering conditions for the mother. And this only after adequate medical and spiritual counseling (Exod. 20:13; Job 31:15; Pss. 22:9; 139:3-16; Isa. 44:2, 24; 49:5; Luke 1:23-25, 36-45; Rom. 12:1-2; 1 Cor. 6:16; 7:1 ff.; 1 Thess. 4:3-6).

Homosexuality. We recognize the physical, psychological, and social pressures and perversions that lead individuals into a practice of homosexuality. Yet we affirm the biblical position that such acts are sinful (Gen. 1:27; 19:1-25; Lev. 20:13; Rom. 1:26-27; 1 Cor. 6:9-11; 1 Tim. 1:8-10). We also believe that God's grace is sufficient to overcome the practice of homosexuality. We believe that His love is for all people. We believe that God can redeem and restore (1 Cor. 6:9-11).

Drug Abuse and Addiction. Many in our society have grown dependent on the use of drugs and stimulants. As a church, we take a *social stand* against such misuse and abuse by abstaining from practice. For the sake of this generation and future generations, we protest the misuse and abuse of drugs in their various forms:

- *Drug abuse.* We stand against the use of unprescribed hallucinogenics, stimulants, and depressants, and the misuse and abuse of regularly prescribed medicines. Only on competent medical advice and under medical supervision should drugs be used.
- *Alcoholic beverages.* We realize that wine was used as a beverage in Bible times (it was often diluted with water in order to provide a purified beverage). However, the use of alcoholic beverages has caused tremendous destruction, death, and despair to millions of people ranging from unborn babies to the aged. Therefore,

  —We serve unfermented wine at the Lord's Supper.

  —No alcoholic beverages are used at any church functions.

  —Our people join this protest by abstaining from the

use of alcoholic beverages (Prov. 20:1; 23:29—24:2; Hos. 4:10-11; Hab. 2:5; Rom. 13:8; 14:15-21; 15:1-2; 1 Cor. 3:16-17; 6:9-12, 19-20; 10:31-33; Gal. 5:13-14, 21; Eph. 5:18).

- *Tobacco.* The Scripture teaches "that you yourselves are God's temple and that God's Spirit lives in you" (1 Cor. 3:16). We are not to destroy God's temple but to treat it with respect, care, and good sense. The use of tobacco is dangerous to the health of people of all ages. It can be addictive and detrimental to individuals and to our culture. Therefore, our people abstain from the use of tobacco.

Guidelines and Helps

Dr. Bresee called these "special advices." Today, they are part of the church's Covenant of Christian Conduct under the heading of the *Christian Life.* The *Manual* states the reasoning for these:

The church joyfully proclaims the good news that we may be delivered from all sin to a new life in Christ. By the grace of God we Christians are to "put off [the] old self"—the old patterns of conduct as well as the old carnal mind—and are to "put on the new self"—a new and holy way of life as well as the mind of Christ. (Ephesians 4:17-24)

The Church of the Nazarene purposes to relate timeless biblical principles to contemporary society in such a way that the doctrines and rules of the church may be known and understood in many lands and within a variety of cultures. We hold that the Ten Commandments, as reaffirmed in the New Testament, constitute the basic Christian ethic and ought to be obeyed in all particulars.

It is further recognized that there is validity in the concept of the collective Christian conscience as illuminated and guided by the Holy Spirit. The Church of the Nazarene, as an international expression of the Body of Christ, acknowledges its responsibility to seek ways to particularize the Christian life so as to lead to a holiness ethic. The historic ethical standards of the church are expressed in part in the following items. They should be followed carefully and conscientiously as guides and helps to holy living. Those who violate the conscience of the church do so at their own peril and to the hurt of the witness of the church. Culturally conditioned adaptations shall be referred to and approved by the Board of General Superintendents.

In listing practices to be avoided we recognize that no catalog, however inclusive, can hope to encompass all forms of evil throughout the world. Therefore it is imperative that our people earnestly seek the aid of the Spirit in cultivating a sensitivity to evil that transcends the mere letter of the law; remembering the admonition: "Test everything. Hold on to the good. Avoid every kind of evil." (1 Thessalonians 5:21-22)

Our leaders and pastors are expected to give strong emphasis in our periodicals and from our pulpits to such fundamental biblical truths as will develop the faculty of discrimination between the evil and the good.

In dealing with special guidelines there are three concepts we must keep in mind: (1) guidelines and helps are instructive and not legalistic; (2) the church family is to encourage, not enforce legalistically; (3) a church member is to follow the guidelines conscientiously, not legalistically.

For a practical example of the dangers of legalism, read the material at the close of this chapter titled "A Warning from History."

In other words, these special helps are to be shared in love. We believe that the following practices should be avoided:

1. *Games of chance that are detrimental to good stewardship and spiritual growth.* Much of the gambling industry is tied to underworld crime. Even government-approved lotteries can create a "fatalistic" attitude and outlook.

2. *Membership in organizations that hurt the Christian's witness and openness.* There are some quasi-religious organizations that demand so much secrecy as to be contrary to the Christian concept of openness and transparency. There is the potential of these groups becoming more prominent in an individual's life than service and commitment to the kingdom of God.

3. *All forms of dancing that promote the sensual and promiscuous.* References to the dance in the Bible are (with a

few exceptions) in relation to celebrative rejoicing and worship (see Exod. 15:20; Pss. 30:11; 149:3). In today's culture, however, the general context for dancing is in social gatherings where wholesome interaction between the sexes often can be eroded. Such situations place an individual in tension between the highest quality of life and relationships desired by a Christian and social pressure to conform to lesser standards of morality and behavior.

4. *Entertainments that promote the pornographic, the violent, and the undermining of Christian living.* In choosing our entertainment, there are three excellent principles to consider: *(a)* the Christian stewardship of leisure time, *(b)* encouraging the best in Christian living and learning, and *(c)* avoiding what would be detrimental to Christian experience. We particularly advise our people concerning the motion picture industry. Many video presentations, motion pictures, and theatrical performances undermine the Christian life and home by promoting the violent, the pornographic, and the obscene.

As you consider the application of these guidelines and helps to your own life, pray that God will help you through His Holy Spirit. He wants your life to be positive, productive, and molded to His image. He does not want you to "conform any longer to the pattern of this world, but be transformed by the renewing of your mind. Then you will be able to test and approve what God's will is—his good, pleasing and perfect will" (Rom. 12:2). You must discover God's will for you. His will is that you become the best Christian you can be. As you make these decisions, let us encourage you with this passage of Scripture: "Let the peace of Christ rule in your hearts, since as members of one body you were called to peace. . . . Let the word of Christ dwell in you richly as you teach and admonish one another with all wisdom. . . . And whatever you do, whether in word or deed, do it all in the name of the Lord Jesus, giving thanks to God the Father through him" (Col. 3:15-17).

The Christ-filled Goal of Discipline

The Scriptures teach, "But solid food is for the mature, who by constant use have trained themselves to distinguish good from evil" (Heb. 5:14).

Righteous living is a process. It takes training. It takes time with Jesus. General Superintendent Roy T. Williams said: "The deepening of the devotional life . . . is the most effective protection against every danger, such as formality, legalism, Pharisaism, worldliness, and sin."

Christian discipleship begins when we "fix our eyes on Jesus, the author and perfecter of our faith" (Heb. 12:2). The plain teaching of Scripture, the practical guidance of mature Christians, and the inner prompting of the Holy Spirit will guide you into becoming a living reminder of the presence of Christ. Jesus took a group of negative, discouraged, and hurt-filled people and turned them into positive, encouraged, helpful human beings. It is the power of Christ, His faith, hope, and love that makes this possible for you. To pursue the meaning and concrete realization of this is discipleship.

General Superintendent Hardy C. Powers beautifully summarized the concept of discipline for the Christian when he said:

> But our final and ultimate safety lies, not in a multiplicity of rules, but in strong love. Jesus said, "If you love me, keep my commandments." And again, "If he loves me, he will keep my words." Christ, in pointing out this truth to Peter, asked him the "heart probing" question, "Do you love me?"
>
> He then went on to declare that upon the purity and strength of perfect love for Christ, we can find the strength and usefulness of the church. (General Assembly, 1952)

A Warning from History

The development of rules, regulations, and rigidity became part of many different churches and denominations in the '30s, '40s, and '50s. Consider the pattern of events that led to a bent toward legalism in many evangelical churches:

The First Generation formed the church through a deep personal experience. Perfect love was expressed in spontaneous joy, excitement, fellowship, and Christian living. They called it "getting the glory down." The same joy, spontaneity, and perfect love is what God's people are looking for today.

74

The Second Generation (1930s) was frightened when the founders began to pass away. The difficulty of the Roaring Twenties, the depression, and war years gave rise to anxiety and fear that the "glory" would be lost. Churches came to define the "glory" as *(a)* loyalty, *(b)* rigid adherence to regulations, and *(c)* demonstrations of emotional outbursts. This kind of religion was popular and prevalent throughout these years. (See *Called unto Holiness,* vol. 1, 294-97.)

At this important time in our history, a great man of God, General Superintendent R. T. Williams, said at the General Assembly in 1940, as a warning against legalism:

> Legalism is the enemy to be feared. Legalism gives more attention to the law than it does to human beings. It emphasizes the letter of the law. In other words, it is law without love. No church can survive unless it fulfills the law of love, both in experience and practice. The Church of the Nazarene operates under grace, backed by law. Legalism would draw us away from grace and put the entire emphasis of the ministry and of ethics upon the matter of law, without mercy and without love. This is a danger ever to be guarded against by the church. (*Called unto Holiness,* vol. 2, 269)

The Third Generation is called to bring the church back to an era of spontaneity, joy, and the free and easy movement of the Spirit, and the guidance of the Holy Spirit in everyday life and conduct. We must learn to have unity in essentials and liberty in nonessentials.

6

What It Means to Be a Church Member

The prayer of a wonderful pastor, Paul, is:

> For this reason I kneel before the Father, from whom his whole family in heaven and on earth derives its name. I pray that out of his glorious riches he may strengthen you with power through his Spirit in your inner being, so that Christ may dwell in your hearts through faith. And I pray that you, being rooted and established in love, may have power, together with all the saints, to grasp how wide and long and high and deep is the love of Christ, and to know this love that surpasses knowledge—that you may be filled to the measure of all the fullness of God *(Eph. 3:14-19).*

This is truly the prayer of your pastor: "to know for yourselves that love so far above our understanding. So will you be filled through all your being with God himself!" (Eph. 3:19, PHILLIPS).

May God fill you with love as *you learn to think as God thinks.* God tells us, "My thoughts are not your thoughts, neither are your ways my ways" (Isa. 55:8). Yet He sent Jesus Christ to live among us. And "we have the mind of Christ" (1 Cor. 2:16).

We are praying that God's love will fill you as you *learn to sense the power of God.* It is possible for you "to know the strength of the Spirit's inner re-inforcement" (Eph. 3:16, PHILLIPS). Jesus promises that "you will receive power when the Holy Spirit comes on you" (Acts 1:8).

It is also our prayer that you will discover God's perfect love as you *learn to do the work of God.* God has included us in His plans. Jesus said, "You will be my witnesses" (Acts 1:8). God's love is worked out in our lives when we discover that He "has made us to be a kingdom and priests to serve" (Rev. 1:6).

A Church of Opportunity

As you become a member of the church, it is our hope and prayer that this family of believers will provide you with opportunities to discover the fullness of God's love in your life. Here are four general areas of opportunity within God's family.

An Opportunity to Grow as a Christian

We are here as a church "so that the body of Christ may be built up until we all reach unity in the faith and in the knowledge of the Son of God and become mature, attaining to the whole measure of the fullness of Christ" (Eph. 4:12-13). As you grow in Jesus, consider the following opportunities:

A Time of Personal Devotion and Quietness. Perhaps the most important source of personal growth is a time of personal quiet and devotion. You may already be involved in a time of daily devotion with God. However, if you would like to begin a "quiet time," let us encourage you to examine the supplement at the end of this chapter titled "How to Develop a Quiet Time."

The Encouragement of Public Worship. We believe in public worship. Music, the preaching of the Word, and meeting with one another on the Lord's Day are vital to the growth of every Christian. The Early Church "continued to meet together in the temple courts. They broke bread in their homes and ate together with glad and sincere hearts, praising God and enjoying the favor of all the people" (Acts 2:46-47).

The Possibilities of Christian Education. We also learn in the Early Church that "they devoted themselves to the apostles' teaching and to the fellowship" (Acts 2:42). There are many ways to get involved in Christian education. We would recommend our Sunday School. There are classes for every age and interest. Also, the midweek service is a "Church Family Night." Everyone is welcome.

Possibilities of a Positive Lifestyle. We want to "be mutually encouraged by each other's faith" (Rom. 1:12). In a world filled with many negatives, we want to offer a positive lifestyle in God's love. We become like the people we associate with. We pray that we will all be people with high standards of conduct and attitudes as we lift one another.

An Opportunity to Serve as a Christian

One of the key verses in the New Testament concerning the Church is: "It was he who gave some to be apostles, some to be prophets, some to be evangelists, and some to be pastors and teachers, to prepare God's people for works of service" (Eph. 4:11-12). It is our firm belief that you are called to serve.

Everyone Is a Minister. The pastor ministers from the pulpit. Others minister as they teach Sunday School. Some share their ministry in opening their homes to friends and neighbors. Others minister in teaching the love of God to their own children. Some are involved in visiting the sick or those in prison, feeding the hungry, or giving to the cause of world missions. The list is as long as our imaginations. The possibilities are as great as human need. To be a minister means *to find a need and fill it with the love of God.*

You Are Called to Minister. God could have chosen to advance His kingdom without our help. God could have chosen a select few to whom to give the task of ministry. In His great wisdom and love, however, God has given all of us an opportunity to serve. If we are born of God, we are born to minister.

You Are Created to Serve. The Bible teaches us that "to each one the manifestation of the Spirit is given for the common good" (1 Cor. 12:7). God has given certain graces, talents, and gifts to each of us. In addition to this, we must work hard at training, developing discipline, and learning to commit ourselves to serving others in the name of Christ. We know that He "has made us to be a kingdom and priests to serve" (Rev. 1:6).

You Are Commissioned to Serve. Jesus began the sending process when He said, "As the Father has sent me, I am sending you" (John 20:21). This church believes in setting people free to serve. We want you to find fulfillment in your service to Christ and His people. We want to support your ministry in the cause of God's kingdom.

If you would like some help in discovering a ministry in

which you could be involved, let us suggest that you look at the supplement titled "How to Find Your Ministry" at the end of this chapter. As you prayerfully consider the five areas, God will begin to reveal a direction of service for you. God has an opportunity for you to serve.

An Opportunity to Give as a Christian

The Bible says, "But just as you excel in everything—in faith, in speech, in knowledge, in complete earnestness and in your love for us—see that you also excel in this grace of giving" (2 Cor. 8:7). Our church wants to provide an opportunity to give to the work of God's kingdom, here and around the world.

Consistent Giving. We want to provide our members with an opportunity to give consistently to God's work. We believe that: "On the first day of every week, each one of you should set aside a sum of money in keeping with his income" (1 Cor. 16:2). We are a tithing church.

Mission Giving. We place in high priority our commitment to world missions. We believe it provides us with an opportunity to expand our vision, share in the needs of others, and experience giving that is a sacrifice. "They gave not only what they could afford, but far more; and I can testify that they did it because they wanted to" (2 Cor. 8:3, TLB). Each year we have opportunities to give to the cause of world missions through the Church of the Nazarene.

Special Giving. We also have opportunities to give to special projects. From time to time, you may feel a desire to do so. "They faithfully brought in the contributions, tithes and dedicated gifts" (2 Chron. 31:12). You may see a need in the church to which you would like to contribute. You may see a ministry that you would like to develop through extra financial support.

An Opportunity to Share Your Faith as a Christian

Many soul winners love the verse of Scripture that says, "The first thing Andrew did was to find his brother Simon and tell him, 'We have found the Messiah'" (John 1:41). One of the greatest opportunities we have as Christians is to share our faith with others. May we encourage you to do so. There are several principles of sharing the faith:

- We have the opportunity and responsibility to share our faith in Christ with others.
- The way we share Christ as a church (through the preaching, singing, and activities) is basic to the way we share Christ individually in our homes and neighborhoods.
- Remember, most people hear of Jesus Christ for the first time outside of the church.
- We share the love of Christ and our faith in Him by meeting the needs of the whole person, including the members of the family.
- There are some who are especially gifted and able to share their faith in a personal way; yet we are all encouraged to tell others of Jesus.
- New believers and new members of a church are often the ones who have more opportunity than anyone else to share their faith.
- Each person must develop a method of sharing his faith that is fulfilling and meaningful.

It is our desire to be a New Testament church of which it was said, "I thank my God through Jesus Christ for all of you, because your faith is being reported all over the world" (Rom. 1:8). We proclaim our faith in Christ when:

- We invite family or friends to attend church with us.
- We share the good things that are happening in our church and our lives with others.
- We take a plate of cookies to a neighbor or listen to a lonely individual.
- We help a friend paint his garage on a Saturday afternoon.
- We pray with someone who is going through a time of difficulty or sickness.
- We share with others how they can turn and trust in Jesus.
- We tell someone what Jesus has done in our lives.

The list goes on and on. God has given many opportunities to share our faith with others. This is one of the greatest joys of being a Christian.

A Church of Responsibility

As you become a member of the Church of the Nazarene, there are four areas of responsibility that we present to you.

We pray that they will lift and encourage you in your Christian walk. We pray that you will join us as we lift up Christ and He draws others to himself.

A Commitment to Personal Growth. We ask our members to commit themselves to personal growth as they attend the worship services, take part in educational opportunities, and develop a positive lifestyle in Jesus Christ.

A Commitment to Ministry. We ask each of our members to find a place of ministry and service in the church. This may be a formal ministry such as music, teaching, and visiting, or an informal ministry of inviting neighbors, showing concern, writing notes of appreciation, and encouraging others. Open your life for God's use wherever you are.

A Commitment to Consistent Giving. We ask our members to give consistently to the work of the church. We are completely dependent upon the gifts of members and friends. When we hear someone say, "We are the Church," this includes each of us.

A Commitment to Share Your Faith. We ask our members to share the faith, hope, and love of Christ with others. There are many ways to do this. The best way is through your own enthusiasm and joy. Let us encourage each of you to invite a friend.

These responsibilities are great. And they are something we do together. They are something we do through mutual encouragement. They are something we do through the love and power of Jesus Christ who said, "For my yoke is easy and my burden is light" (Matt. 11:30). In Jesus, the burden becomes a blessing and a journey is a joy.

Joining the Church of the Nazarene

You are ready to become a member of the Church of the Nazarene. Let us be the first to welcome you. We love you. The procedure for membership is simple.

- Follow the procedures and fill out the forms required for your local church.
- You may have an area of ministry in which you are interested. Please indicate this to your pastor or a church leader. Also, if you have any questions concerning your Sunday School class or other ministries, indicate these.

- If you are received publicly into the church family, may we encourage you to invite friends and relatives for this special service.

There may be other questions you have. It would be impossible to answer them all in a written form. However, these are some of the most common questions that people ask as they are preparing for membership.

- *Do my children join with me?* The Church of the Nazarene has no age limit for membership. If your children have been converted to Christ and have the desire to join, they may join with you. Many families join together. However, your children may join separately also.
- *What about being baptized?* Baptism and membership are separate in our church. If you have been baptized and are satisfied with your baptism, this is sufficient. However, if you have not been baptized, there are opportunities for baptism. You are invited to participate.
- *What about transferring my membership?* If you are transferring your membership from another Church of the Nazarene or another denomination, indicate this on the "Welcome to Membership" form. The pastor will write a letter asking for your transfer.

A Personal Word

"What does it mean to be a church member?" Joining the church does not change our status before God. However, it does say something about our commitment to one another. Becoming a member of the church is saying, "I will serve my Lord and Savior, Jesus Christ, with this local family of God."

We believe that God has great things in store for the church. And we believe He has good things in store for you. "Now to him who is able to do immeasurably more than all we ask or imagine, according to his power that is at work within us, to him be glory in the church and in Christ Jesus throughout all generations, for ever and ever! Amen" (Eph. 3:20-21).

How to Develop a Quiet Time

(Adapted from *Seven Minutes with God*, by Robert B. Foster)

In 1882 on the campus of Cambridge University the world was first given the slogan: "Remember the morning watch."

Students like Hooper and Thornton found their days loaded with studies, lectures, games, and bull sessions. Enthusiasm and activity were the order of the day. These dedicated men soon discovered a flaw in their spiritual armor, a small crack that, if not soon closed, would bring disaster.

They sought an answer and came up with a scheme they called the morning watch, a plan to spend the first minutes of a new day alone with God, praying and reading the Bible.

The morning watch sealed the crack. It enshrined a truth so often obscured by the pressure of ceaseless activity that it needs daily rediscovery: To know God, it is necessary to spend consistent time with Him.

The idea caught fire: "A remarkable period of religious blessing" followed and culminated in the departure of the Cambridge Seven, a band of prominent athletes and men of wealth and education, for missionary service. They gave up everything to go to China for Christ.

But these men found that getting out of bed in time for the morning watch was as difficult as it was vital. Thornton was determined to turn indolence into discipline. He invented an automatic, foolproof cure for laziness. It was a contraption set up by his bed. "The vibration of an alarm clock set fishing tackle in motion, and the sheets, clipped to the line, moved swiftly into the air off the sleeper's body."

Thornton wanted to get up to meet his God!

The intimacy of communion with Christ must be recaptured in the morning quiet time. Call it what you want—the quiet time, personal devotions, the morning watch, or individual worship—these holy minutes at the start of each day explain the inner secret of Christianity. It's the golden thread that ties every great man of God together, from Moses to David Livingstone, the prophet Amos to Billy Graham, rich and poor, businessmen and military personnel. Every man who ever became somebody for God has at this core of his priorities: Time alone with God!

David says in Ps. 57:7, "My heart is fixed, O God, my heart is fixed" (KJV). A fixed and established heart produces stability in life. Few men in the Christian community have this heart and life. One of the missing links has been a workable plan on how to begin and maintain a morning watch.

I want to suggest that, in order to get under way, you start with seven minutes. Perhaps you could call it a daily "Seven Up." Five minutes may be too short, and 10 minutes for some is a little too long at first.

Are you willing to take seven minutes every morning? Not five mornings out of seven, not six days out of seven—but seven days out of seven! Ask God to help you: "Lord, I want to meet You first thing in the morning for at least seven minutes. Tomorrow when the alarm clock goes off at 6:15 A.M., I have an appointment with You."

Your prayer might be, "In the morning, O LORD, you hear my voice; in the morning I lay my requests before you and wait in expectation" (Ps. 5:3).

How do you spend these seven minutes? After getting out of bed and taking care of your personal needs, you will want to find a quiet place and there, with your Bible, enjoy the solitude of seven minutes with God.

Invest the first minutes preparing your heart. Thank Him for the good night of sleep and the opportunities of this new day. "Lord, cleanse my heart so that You can speak to me through the Scriptures. Open my heart. Fill my heart. Make my mind alert, my soul active, and my heart responsive. Lord, surround me with Your presence during this time. Amen."

Now take four minutes to read the Bible. Your greatest need is to hear some word from God. Allow the Word to strike fire in your heart. Meet the Author!

One of the Gospels is a good place to begin reading. Start with the Book of Mark. Read consecutively—verse after verse, chapter after chapter. Don't race, but avoid stopping to do a Bible study on some word, thought, or theological problem that presents itself. Read for the pure joy of reading and allowing God to speak—perhaps just 20 verses, or maybe a complete chapter. When you have finished Mark, start with the Gospel of John. Soon you'll want to go ahead and read the entire New Testament.

After God has spoken through His Book, then speak to Him in prayer. You now have two minutes left for fellowship with Him in prayer.

Let's put these seven minutes together:

1 minute	Prayer for guidance (Ps. 143:8)
4 minutes	Reading the Bible (Ps. 119:18)
<u>2 minutes</u>	Prayer
7 minutes	

May God enrich your relationship with Him as you give Him the beginning of each day.

How to Find Your Ministry

Finding a ministry that is personally fulfilling, of service to the Kingdom, and anointed by God's Spirit takes time, maturity, wise counsel, and good sense under the direction of God. This survey will help you in your quest.

Fill out as much of the survey as you can now, then refer to it again and again. May God give you direction and a sense of confidence. *You are a minister!* God has a ministry for you!

I. *Willing to Try.* Check the record. List the ministries and places of service you have tried, indicating the results (3—Good; 2—Fair; 1—Poor; 0—Rather not talk about it).

II. *Set Your Goal.* Look at the desires of your heart. What would you like to do in ministry and service to others? Think: **If you could do anything for God and knew that you couldn't fail, what would you desire to do?**

C. _____ _ _ _ _

D. _____ _ _ _ _

E. _____ _ _ _ _

F. _____ _ _ _ _

III. *Sense the Needs.* Turn from looking at your own goals to the needs around you. What do you see as the most pressing needs in our church? (The needs you see are often a reflection of the gifts God has given you and the ministry He has called you to.)

A. _____

B. _____

C. _____

D. _____

E. _____

F. _____

IV. *Look for Opportunities (Possibilities).* When God gives a dream, He will open a door. What are the opportunities for service around you? List the possibilities.

A. _____

B. _____

C. _____

D. _____

E. _____

F. _____

V. *Listen for Affirmation.* The Holy Spirit affirms ministry. He does this in the "temple of your own spirit" in moments of prayer or worship or meditation (Bible study). He also affirms us through the church (God's family) as they complement, counsel, and confirm us.* We will call these two "inward" and "outward" confirmation. Keep a record of the affirmation of the Spirit.

Date	Notes	Inward	Outward
___	_____	___	_____
___	_____	___	_____
___	_____	___	_____
___	_____	___	_____

A Prayer for Direction

Lord, believing that You are leading me, I will pursue my call to ministry by:

Searching Your Word for guidance, reaffirmation through prayer and counsel with the pastor or other spiritual leaders.

I remember that . . .

I am Yours completely!
I am called by You!
I am a minister!

And Lord, this ministry is Yours! May it be to the glory of Jesus and the maturity of Your Church. Amen.

---

*NOTE: Sometimes solid, positive, mature Christians can also help us see that we may be moving in the wrong direction in ministry. Do *not* listen to all negative words, but we must be sensitive to the wise counsel of people we respect spiritually.

7 | Welcome to the Church of the Nazarene

Welcome to the Church of the Nazarene! We believe it is a great church. Some people measure greatness in terms of activity. Other think of a great church as being a *big* church. Still others define greatness in terms of growth or giving or being missionary minded or need centered or smooth running. All of these things are important. However, we have discovered that a great church is made up of a great people. And great people are filled with the love and the glory of God.

A Great Purpose

Every endeavor needs purpose. The Church of the Nazarene also has a central purpose. It has been stated in many ways, but never so succinctly as from the pen of one of our early founders, Phineas F. Bresee. In an editorial from an early publication called *Nazarene Messenger,* he wrote, August 18, 1904: "The Church of the Nazarene has set its face toward the northern star of perfect love and will not swerve to the right or to the left. Side issues are no part of her plan or teaching."

God's perfect love is the center of our preaching and our teaching. Yet it is far more important to have God's perfect love as the center of your heart, your attitudes, and your home. Jesus described the power of perfect love in these words, "As the Father has loved me, so have I loved you. Now remain in my love. . . . This is my command: Love each other" (John 15:9, 17).

A Great Program

A great church, a mature church, has learned to balance a program that involves:

- The Ministry of Evangelism
- The Ministry of Education
- The Ministry of Relationships

Just as the body is carefully balanced in all its functions, the church (this part of the Body of Christ) must also be balanced.

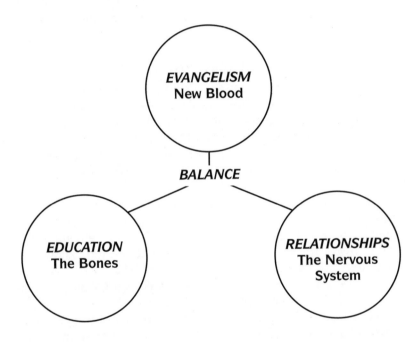

Evangelism is our "open door policy." It is our desire to open the church to everyone who wishes to come. More importantly, it is our desire to open hearts to the love of Jesus Christ.

Education involves a "comprehensive curriculum." We live in an age of great diversity. Therefore, it is essential that our education and learning opportunities in church cover a broad spectrum of needs while being based solidly upon the Word of God. We need to fill our minds and hearts with the Bible.

The *Ministry of Relationships* involves "concern in attitude and action." We need programs that say to our community: "We care." Yet, beyond this, we need people whose hearts respond to the needs of others. We need an attitude that moves us to find a genuine need and fill it with the love of God.

We can think of the church as a body. The *Ministry of Evangelism* brings new blood into the system. The *Ministry of Education* is the bones that give structure and strength. The *Ministry of Relationships* forms the nervous system that keeps us in touch with the joys and hurts of each other. "The body is a unit, though it is made up of many parts; and though all its parts are many, they form one body" (1 Cor. 12:12).

A Great Power

Purpose and program are essential; however, they are useless without power. The New Testament never describes a mature church in terms of its program; however, Scripture does have a definition of maturity for a church.

To the Church at Corinth: "And now these three remain: faith, hope and love. But the greatest of these is love" (1 Cor. 13:13).

To Church at Ephesus: "For this reason, ever since I heard about your faith in the Lord Jesus and your love for all the saints, I have not stopped giving thanks for you, remembering you in my prayers. . . . I pray also . . . that you may know the hope to which he has called you" (Eph. 1:15-16, 18).

To the Church at Colosse: "We always thank God, the Father of our Lord Jesus Christ, when we pray for you, because we have heard of your faith in Christ Jesus and of the love you have for all the saints—the faith and love that spring from the hope that is stored up for you in heaven" (Col. 1:3-5).

To the Church at Thessalonica: "We always thank God for all of you, mentioning you in our prayers. We continually remember before our God and Father your work produced by faith, your labor prompted by love, and your endurance inspired by hope in our Lord Jesus Christ" (1 Thess. 1:2-3).

The measure of a mature church is Faith, Hope, and Love! This is a church that has the power necessary to fulfill its purpose through a balanced program.

Faith in the local church is confidence in Jesus Christ as the true Leader of the church. We believe that He has called us to a great task. We are confident that He is guiding us in the work that He has called us to do. We are so confident that we are willing to obey any command that He may give.

Hope is an optimistic outlook that comes through a deep understanding of God's Word, God's work, and God's will. Hope is developed as we fill our minds and hearts with the living and written Word of God. Hope is matured as we face mountains with stability and perseverance.

Love in the local church is a description of the relationship that exists among the people as a result of God's presence upon them. It is seen in the way we treat one another. Love is what draws a little boy across a snowy city to a church where he can say, "I come because they love a fella around here."

A Great People

You are a great person, and we are thrilled that you are part of the Church of the Nazarene.

The Church of the Nazarene has a mission of love. We gather up the broken, hurting people of the earth and introduce them to the message of the cross of Christ, through the God who loves men and can do for them what they cannot do for themselves.

The Church of the Nazarene matures people in hope. These individuals are continually discussing the Lordship of Christ, which is the base of their lives. Struggles, trials, and temptations mold them into men and women of God. Steadfastness and perseverance are secure as we look forward to the return of Jesus.

The Church of the Nazarene marches forward in faith. With a sense of vision and possibility in the power of God, people are united together under the Lordship of Christ to move out in service and servanthood with the same life power that moved Christ out of a tomb into Easter Sunday.

As you join the church, let us share with you a great charge:

Let us draw near to God with a sincere heart in full assurance of <u>faith</u>, having our hearts sprinkled to cleanse us from a guilty conscience and having our bodies washed with pure water. Let us hold unswervingly to the <u>hope</u> we profess, for he who promised is faithful. And let us consider how we may spur one another on toward <u>love</u> and good deeds. Let us not give up meeting together, as some are in the habit of doing, but let us encourage one another—and all the more as you see the Day approaching *(Heb. 10:22-25).*

Welcome to membership in the Church of the Nazarene. Our church can be your home!

Bibliography

Brickley, Donald P. *Man of the Morning: The Life and Work of Phineas F. Bresee.* Kansas City: Nazarene Publishing House, 1960.

Girvin, E. A. *Phineas F. Bresee: A Prince in Israel, a Biography.* Kansas City: Nazarene Publishing House, 1916.

Purkiser, W. T. *Called unto Holiness.* Vol. 2, *The Second Twenty-five Years, 1933-58.* Kansas City: Nazarene Publishing House, 1983.

Purkiser, W. T., Richard S. Taylor, and Willard H. Taylor. *God, Man, and Salvation: A Biblical Theology.* Kansas City: Beacon Hill Press of Kansas City, 1977.

Smith, Timothy L. *Called unto Holiness.* Vol. 1, *The Formative Years, 1908-33.* Kansas City: Nazarene Publishing House, 1962.

Wesley, John. *A Plain Account of Christian Perfection.* Reprint, Kansas City: Beacon Hill Press of Kansas City, 1966.

Wiley, H. Orton. *Christian Theology.* 3 vols. Kansas City: Beacon Hill Press, 1940-43.